WITHDRAWN

A NEW BOOK OF THE GROTESQUES

ROBERT DUNNE

A New Book of the Grotesques

CONTEMPORARY APPROACHES
TO SHERWOOD ANDERSON'S
EARLY FICTION

THE KENT STATE UNIVERSITY PRESS

KENT AND LONDON

©2005 by The Kent State University Press, Kent, Ohio 44242
Library of Congress Catalog Card Number 2004025483
ISBN 0-87338-827-5
Manufactured in the United States of America
09 08 07 06 05   5 4 3 2 1

Library of Congress Cataloging-in-Publication Data
Dunne, Robert, 1964–
    A new book of the grotesques : contemporary approaches to Sherwood Anderson's
early fiction / Robert Dunne.
        p.   cm.
    Includes bibliographical references and index.
    ISBN 0-87338-827-5 (hardcover : alk. paper) ∞
    1. Anderson, Sherwood, 1876–1941—Criticism and interpretation. 2. Anderson,
Sherwood, 1876–1941. 3. City and town life in literature. 4. Grotesque in literature. 5. Ohio—
In literature. I. Title.
    PS3501.N4Z59 2005
    813'.52—dc22   2004025483

British Library Cataloging-in-Publication data are available.

This one's for you, Mary

CONTENTS

ACKNOWLEDGMENTS

Long in my mind and slowly chipped away at for over a dozen years, this book is a fulfillment of my years of reading and thinking about Sherwood Anderson's works. Finally getting it all down on paper, however, would not have been possible without the sabbatical leave that Central Connecticut State University awarded me in 2000. Several other research grants, as well as time made available by Central for the project, are also gratefully acknowledged.

I wish also to thank the staff at Central's Elihu Burritt Library, especially at the interlibrary loan office, for their help and expeditious service.

Portions of this book had trial runs as conference papers at the annual meetings of the Modern Language Association, the Midwest Modern Language Association, the American Literature Association, and the Society for the Study of Midwestern Literature; I would like to thank the many scholars of Sherwood Anderson who provided constructive comments.

Students in two graduate seminars, Sherwood Anderson and Some Cross-Currents of Modernism, and Narrative Duplicity in the American Short Story, as well as students in my course on Modern American Literature, provided many fine insights.

I want especially to thank Mary M. Bellor, whose timely help in the home-stretch allowed me to finish revising the manuscript, and the staff at the Kent State University Press for its expert guidance in preparing the manuscript for publication.

Finally, endless gratitude goes to my wife, Mary—partner, friend, fellow new parent, and longtime supporter of this project. Cheers, kid!

Introduction

SHERWOOD ANDERSON'S PLACE
IN A MILLENNIAL CANON

> The time will come when . . . there will be a renaissance and
> then my own work and my own life will be appreciated.
> SHERWOOD ANDERSON

During his lifetime, Herman Melville was well aware of the significance that a literary reputation had in his culture and also particularly aware of his own standing among his peers. In the midst of writing *Moby-Dick* he lamented his reputation to Nathaniel Hawthorne: "Think of it! To go down to posterity is bad enough, any way; but to go down as a 'man who lived among the cannibals'!"[1] Indeed, at the time of his death in 1891, if Melville was remembered at all it was for such works as *Typee* and *Omoo,* not for *Moby-Dick* or "Benito Cereno" (*Billy Budd* not yet having been published).

Only after Melville was rediscovered in the 1920s did his standing in the American literary canon shift from a marginalized corner to a place of central importance, where it has comfortably rested to the present day. But his reputation has not remained static. Throughout the twentieth and into the twenty-first century, each generation of critics has found a "new" Melville who merits his preeminent place in the canon. As Paul Lauter has ably shown, critics in the early 1920s embraced the Melville who shunned genteel American culture;[2] later in the 1920s other critics loved the Melville who was a forerunner of Freud; by World War II critics had discovered the fiercely democratic Melville; and in the last thirty years, Marxist critics, African Americanists, poststructuralists, and queer-studies critics have heralded their Melville. Melville's works have of course remained the same, yet the *reasons* for his secure standing in the canon have been as varied as the critical temperament of each generation that has examined him.

The history of Melville's critical reputation serves as an apt illustration for the motivation behind this book: locating Sherwood Anderson's place in an expanding American literary canon. Now, few would argue that Anderson's work merits as high a regard as Melville's. And perhaps fewer still should be concerned that Anderson is in danger of being omitted entirely by the practical guardians of the canon: writers of literary histories, editors of literature anthologies, and professors of college courses in American literature. In fact, Anderson enjoyed a fairly esteemed reputation during his lifetime (which Melville did not), one that has not abated since he died in 1941. But what concerns me here is that the *variety* of critical perspectives that has sustained Melville's reputation through the years is lacking for Anderson, especially now as today's generation of critics rediscovers and introduces more and more writers into the canon. Anderson's significance in Midwestern circles has always loomed large, but his position in the wider American literary canon has never been at the center, and in the current academic and critical climate, that position is in danger of becoming even more insignificant.[3] But need it be?

As noted, unlike Melville, Anderson gained entrance into the canon when he was still alive. As early as 1926, Doubleday's American literature anthology included several *Winesburg* tales: "A Man of Ideas," "'Queer,'" and "Drink." Even when Anderson's reputation was on the wane in the 1930s, another anthology, *The American Mind* (1937), lavished him with two sets of entries, including "An Apology for Crudity" in a section on literary criticism and "I'm a Fool" under the section "Recent Trends in Fiction." Two years later the austere *Oxford Anthology of American Literature* included one story, "Death in the Woods." At the time of his death in 1941, the first anthology of American literature published by D. C. Heath also included "I'm a Fool."[4]

Anderson's steady appearance in American literature anthologies continued throughout the 1940s and 1950s. Usually these collections limited his inclusion to a single short story: "Death in the Woods" in Scribner's anthology of 1949; "'Queer'" in another Heath anthology and arranged thematically under "The Revolt of the Individual"; and "I Want to Know Why" in the first Norton anthology of American literature.[5]

If we accept literature anthologies as a valid gauge of an author's place in the canon, then Anderson attained his most significant place in it as a result of Perry Miller's influential *Major Writers of America* anthology (1962).[6] Grouped with Fitzgerald and Hemingway, Anderson received lengthy biographical treatment by Mark Schorer and the inclusion of three stories ("The Book of the Grotesque," "The Egg," and "I Want to Know Why"); excerpts from *A Story Teller's Story*; his sketches "Four American Impressions"; and twelve letters. Only twenty-seven authors are included in this two-volume anthology, which ranges in chronology from William Bradford to William Faulkner. Thus Anderson found himself in rather exclusive company.

Approaching our present time, however, Anderson's representation has again been limited to one short story, in many cases—although the *Norton Anthology of American Literature* from its inception in 1979 (Gottesman) up to its 1998 edition (Baym) had been very generous, including four *Winesburg* tales. The Little, Brown anthology of 1970 (Poirier) includes only the story "I Want to Know Why," and the current Prentice Hall *Anthology of American Literature* (McMichael) also includes just one tale ("Death in the Woods"). The most recent anthologies have moved in opposing directions, with the latest edition of the *Heath Anthology of American Literature* (Lauter) doubling the number of entries by Anderson from its previous edition to two works ("Hands" and "Death in the Woods") and the 2002 *Norton* scaling back to three: "Mother," "Adventure," and "'Queer'" (Baym).[7]

As this brief survey demonstrates, Anderson has never garnered the kind of attention that a Hawthorne or a Faulkner has; in anthologies from the 1930s up to the present his representation has often been limited to a single short story. So someone might ask me, "What's your point? He's receiving the same kind of attention now as he generally did when he was alive. How then is his place in the canon threatened?" I contend that his place in the canon is becoming less significant for this reason: the first American literature anthologies typically were one thousand to fifteen hundred pages in length, but the recent ones, particularly the *Heath*, run to well over three thousand pages. The inclusion of a dozen or so pages by Anderson in today's anthologies carries less weight and presence than it once did.

As today's leading anthologies—especially the *Heath* but also Prentice Hall's and the *Norton*—attempt to be more representative of America's multicultural heritage, they are faced with the challenge of expanding their inclusion of authors while at the same time keeping the number of pages within realistic bounds. If this trend continues, Sherwood Anderson's significance in American literary history will surely be reduced because, literally, he will become lost in the crowd.

But if multiculturalism (or the broader term, cultural studies) has become the standard methodology by which editors of today's anthologies and literary histories evaluate American authors, then there is indeed hope for Sherwood Anderson. For most of the twentieth century, New Criticism was the most influential methodology scholars used to interpret literature. With its emphasis on examining the artistic and aesthetic qualities of a literary work, New Criticism pays more attention to *how* a text means rather than to *what* it means. Put another way, New Criticism focuses on the supposedly intrinsic qualities of a literary work rather than on the social issues a work addresses or other matters that historically situate that work.

As a result of this dominant critical perspective, it is little wonder that Anderson has always held a stable, but minor, place in the American canon. What early anthologies and literary histories emphasized about Anderson were generally his innovations in the short-story form and his influence on later generations of writers. But these accolades would usually be qualified by immediate reference to his larger "artistic" flaws, particularly in the all-important novelistic form. For instance, Russell Blankenship in an anthology published in 1931 states that Anderson "is never brilliant, and indeed succeeds only occasionally." And George Whicher, writing in *The Literature of the American People* (1951), says, "The writer's talent . . . was not well adapted to the rigorous discipline that the construction of novels demands." Even in Perry Miller's *Major Writers of America,* the anthology that showcased Anderson's work more extensively than any other, Anderson is criticized by Mark Schorer for squandering his talent on poorly constructed novels: "Over and over he would attempt the longer form of the novel where, over and over, he would lose his imaginative grip on his materials."[8]

Judged according to the criteria of New Criticism, then, Anderson's primary importance to American literary history rested on his artistic innovations in the short story, a form that has never had the kind of esteem among critics as has the novel. Robert Spiller's seminal *Literary History of the United States* cites Anderson's achievements in the shorter form: "[Anderson's] place in American literary history should be given further distinction by his very great influence in liberating the American short story from a petrifying technique."[9] But artistic form and other aesthetic niceties are no longer of central importance to today's critics, who look beyond merely artistic evaluations of works in determining what is "in" and what is "out." One might wonder why Anderson has not benefited as a result.

The reason cannot be because Anderson's works are not in print. Within the last fifteen or so years alone there have been a dozen new editions of the fiction and nonfiction originally published during his lifetime, including *Kit Brandon, Poor White, A Story Teller's Story, The Triumph of the Egg*, and *Windy McPherson's Son*, and in the last decade seven different editions of *Winesburg, Ohio*.[10] Rounding out the new editions of Anderson's fiction is Charles E. Modlin's selection of Anderson's short stories, *Certain Things Last* (also published under the title *The Egg and Other Stories*). In addition, Modlin (*Sherwood Anderson's Love Letters*) and Modlin with Welford Dunaway Taylor (*Southern Odyssey: Selected Writings by Sherwood Anderson*), as well as Hilbert H. Campbell, William Sutton, and Ray Lewis White, have edited a substantial amount of Anderson's unpublished work, including his early business writings, diaries, and even love letters to his wife. Probably not since he was alive have so many of Anderson's works been in print at one time.

And yet the paradox remains that despite the availability in print of so many of Anderson's works, indicating his continuing significance for the reading public, his presence in anthologies and literary histories is becoming increasingly marginalized. As a case in point, the *Columbia Literary History of the United States* (1988) is one of the most recent comprehensive literary histories in print. Arranged thematically, not chronologically, the *Columbia Literary History* provides chapter-length treatment on such literary luminaries as Melville, Dickinson, Twain, James, and Faulkner, among others, but provides only glancing references to Anderson, touching on *Winesburg*, mentioning Anderson's short-lived attraction to the Communist Party, and including reference to *Dark Laughter* in a discussion on antifeminism in early twentieth-century writers. There is hardly a paragraph that assesses Anderson's career at length. And perhaps reflecting its multicultural methodology and abandonment of New Criticism, there are none of the by-now perfunctory comments on Anderson's experiments in the short story and his failures in novel-writing. The *Columbia*'s scant treatment raises new and disturbing questions, though. If Anderson was regarded only with qualified esteem for most of the twentieth century because he did not pass muster when the dominant New Criticism held sway, the *Columbia Literary History* and recent anthologies do not give any indication that his reputation is improving in the present age of cultural studies and poststructuralism.[11]

In a recent review of Judy Jo Small's *Reader's Guide* to Anderson's short stories, Stephen Ennis hits on the current dilemma surrounding Anderson's reputation and hints at some possible solutions. He writes: "As is inevitable with such a work, this survey of biographical and critical material is inherently backward looking. In this post-modernist age, do we really need to continue to review arguments over the unity of *Winesburg, Ohio* one might ask?"[12] Ennis is on to something here. There has been a superabundance of biographical, New Critical, and psychoanalytic work done on Anderson—much of which has been insightful, informative, and genuinely rewarding for anyone interested in his life and work. This core criticism has kept Anderson's work in circulation and his reputation intact, even when each new generation has had a critic who, like Lionel Trilling, pronounced Anderson as retrograde and finished.

But we also have to admit—as Clarence B. Lindsay has noticed—that Anderson scholarship has not adequately tapped into some of the more recent and innovative theoretical approaches to literature that have, taken as a whole, replaced New Criticism as the industry standard.[13] I have in mind post-structuralist, New Historicist, neo-Marxist, feminist, and multiculturalist approaches, among the many others in circulation. Of course, some applications of these methodologies may be faddish or reactionary and jargon-ridden, but the example of Melville's critical reception should serve as a reminder that Melville's reputation has remained so high because his work has been able to ride the wave of each generation of new critical approaches. Similarly, I contend that there is enough to be found in the corpus of Anderson's work to sustain and enhance his reputation. Anderson's canonical status could very well be the beneficiary as current literary theory moves away from measuring the significance of literary works by "purely" artistic standards and begins to consider matters of race, class, gender, and postmodern conceptions of language and power. In today's literature anthologies and literary histories, Anderson is still the innovator of the modern short story but the bumbling novel writer. But if Anderson scholars can tap into the rich reservoir of newer critical approaches, we will discover, as scholars did with Melville, many "new" Sherwood Andersons. This book does not attempt to provide an exhaustive application of myriad critical approaches; instead, it begins the challenge by applying postmodern theories concerning the indeterminacy of language and Foucauldian power relations to Anderson's earliest fiction, up to and including *Winesburg, Ohio*. Its aims are to open a door previously only ajar to newer, rewarding readings of Anderson, and thus to settle his works securely into the canon of the twenty-first century.

The subject of the grotesque in literature has gotten considerable attention in recent years from scholars working from contemporary theoretical perspectives. Sherwood Anderson, in spite of decades of critical attention to his conception of the grotesque, has received no mention in these works.[14] This is a telling omission, because it suggests that Anderson has been left on the sidelines by scholars trained in the last ten or twenty years. It is also an undeserved omission, because Anderson's works provide a fertile ground for contemporary theory, particularly the early works that focus on the grotesque.

This is especially true when considering Anderson's masterpiece, *Winesburg, Ohio*. Specifically, I see at least two challenges emerging: Anderson's conception of the grotesque and his deceptively simple narrative prose style. In his conceptualization of the grotesque, Anderson refashioned conventional meanings of the term in perceiving the grotesque as a characteristic of the alienation and isolation fostered by a modern, industrial age. Such a perspective is still of interest in our postmodern, information age. And in his narrative prose style, Anderson not only moved away from the plot-driven fiction made popular by O. Henry but also exposed the tenuous foundation of meaning in language, a subject of keen interest to postmodernist thinkers. Anderson scholars have for years grappled with both ideas, frequently from the interpretive vantage points of psychoanalysis, New Criticism, and biographical readings.[15] Relatively few scholars, though, have applied to these issues the interpretive tools provided by postmodern theories. Fresh insights into *Winesburg* and other works by Anderson await anyone who might test such theories on his works. This book attempts a beginning of just such an endeavor.

CHAPTER ONE

Anderson's Grotesques

PERSONAL SUBJUGATION AND THE
INDETERMINACY OF MEANING IN
A HOSTILE WORLD

Up until the late nineteenth century, the concept of the grotesque in the arts and literature had focused predominantly on the fantastic, the macabre, or the supernatural.[1] The grotesque subject bore some resemblance to the "ordinary" but typically in a distorted way so that often the physical features of the subject were frightful or even comically absurd.[2] From the Renaissance into the nineteenth century, the grotesque often converged the mysteries of the spiritual realm with allegorical representations of human depravity. Because the term has covered such expansive ground, it is difficult to pin down neatly a precise meaning of the grotesque in both its characteristics and form. As Geoffrey Galt Harpham has observed, "The grotesque is concept without form: the word nearly always modifies such indeterminate nouns as *monster, object,* or *thing.* As a noun it implies that an object either occupies multiple categories or that it falls between categories."[3] Rather consistently, though, the grotesque subject was objectified as a thing or person deviant from the social norm. It was a freak in a normal world. But by the late nineteenth century, this conception would undergo a change: artists began to perceive the "normal world" as either itself grotesque or a significant cause of a person's becoming grotesque.

As Wolfgang Kayser argues, it is in the late nineteenth century when fiction of the grotesque emerges that is not based on supernatural or fantastic elements but as a result of social phenomena. Both Kayser and Bernard McElroy locate this shift in the work of Russian authors such as Dostoevsky and Gogol; McElroy hails the Russians as forerunners of the modern grotesque.[4] By the

1

end of the century, with the inroads of industrialism and the centralization of political power (contained either in the state or in a capitalistic economy), the role and purpose of the individual were undergoing a change. The romantic conviction in the autonomous powers of the individual was beginning to be seen more and more as the stuff of myth rather than as an attainable possibility.[5] This change would take place so rapidly that by the second decade of the twentieth century, when Sherwood Anderson emerged as an author, the fin de siècle was already regarded as a bygone age in the country's history. But it is in Anderson's early work that we see a crystallization of the modern grotesque.

In the early twentieth century, American authors such as Anderson began to experiment with the concept of the grotesque as a condition of modern life rather than as a fantastic or supernatural phenomenon. This is significant in part because the focus was no longer on the grotesque subject-as-deviant but on modern society's role in either inducing grotesqueness or being grotesque itself. Also, grotesque characteristics were no longer primarily physical but had become sublimated to the psychic realm, where alienation and isolation became its main features. McElroy offers an excellent summation of these features:

> Man is usually presented as living in a vast, indifferent, meaningless universe in which his actions are without significance beyond his own, limited, personal sphere. The physical world of his immediate surroundings is alien and hostile, directing its energies to overwhelming the individual, denying him a place and identity even remotely commensurate with his needs and aspirations, surrounding him on every side with violence and brutalisation, offering him values that have lost their credibility, [and] manipulating and dehumanising him through vast, faceless institutions.[6]

This passage underscores how artists began to regard the individual in modern society as powerless, subject to the apparent whims of far-reaching and anonymous sources of power. From this perspective, Michel Foucault's writings on power and the body can shed valuable insights on both the modern grotesque and Anderson's conception of the grotesque.

In many of Foucault's writings, such as *Discipline and Punish* (1975), *Madness and Civilization* (1961), and *The History of Sexuality* (1976), the French critic analyzes the progressive alienation and powerlessness of the individual from a number of perspectives, focusing on the Renaissance period through the twentieth century. In *Madness and Civilization*, for instance, in which Foucault discusses how Western society has identified and treated the insane, the analogies to the modern grotesque become inescapable. If a recurring characteristic of the traditional grotesque had been deviance from or failure to attain the social norm, then what Foucault says about Western society's treatment of the insane has particular relevance to the modern grotesque.

In describing nineteenth century asylums in Europe, for example, Foucault argues that surveillance and judgment—rather than physical discipline—became the mainstay in ministering to the insane. The madman would be given certain liberties dependent on his good behavior and be informed that his retention of such liberties was contingent entirely on himself. As Foucault states, "The madman . . . must feel morally responsible for everything within him that may disturb morality and society, and must hold no one but himself responsible for the punishment he receives."[7] The individual must subject himself, in other words, to an environment that is watching and evaluating—and subjecting—him. But this watching and evaluating is based only on what can be seen *visibly*. One's interiority must suffer the consequences as one's exterior behavior in society becomes the primary means of validating sanity. For, as Foucault goes on, the individual deemed mad would be placed in formal social situations "where everyone was obliged to imitate all the formal requirements of social existence," whereby "everyone" could observe, or "spy out [in the insane] any incongruity, any disorder, any awkwardness where madness might betray itself."[8] One result for the individual is a constant tension between his outer conformity to social norms and his silenced inner self. As Foucault argues, "Curiously, this rite is not one of intimacy, of dialogue, of mutual acquaintance; it is the organization around the madman of a world where everything would be like and near him, but in which he himself would remain a stranger, the Stranger *par excellence* who is judged not only by appearances but by all that may betray and reveal in spite of themselves."[9] The individual therefore remains alienated from his society, knowing that judgment surrounds his every action; "he must know that he is watched, judged, and condemned." From this societal surveillance and self-surveillance, a "homogenous rule of morality" is preserved and "its rigorous extension [applied] to all those who tend to escape from it."[10]

The combination of surveillance and subjection and the upholding of a normalized morality can be extended from the domain of presumed insanity to others as well. As Foucault details elsewhere, sexuality and labor also fall

3

under this rubric. In *The History of Sexuality* he discusses the repercussions of science overtaking organized religion as the authority on sex during the nineteenth century. Regarding science and its role in treating this subject, Foucault writes, "It concerned itself primarily with aberrations, perversions, exceptional oddities, pathological abatements, and morbid aggravations. It was by the same token a science subordinated in the main to the imperatives of a morality whose divisions it reiterated under the guise of a medical norm." "Sexuality" as a term came into use by science in the nineteenth century as a "domain susceptible to pathological processes, and hence one calling for therapeutic or normalizing interventions."[11] Here, too, another dimension of the individual falls prey to subjection and surveillance, with the goal of preserving a "homogeneous rule of morality."

Elsewhere Foucault argues that the individual's autonomy over his body in the domain of labor is also contingent on similar kinds of control and subjection. In *Discipline and Punish,* for example, he maintains that the individual is deemed useful in society if he is simultaneously productive and constrained:

> But the body is also directly involved in a political field; power relations have an immediate hold upon it; they invest it, mark it, train it, . . . force it to carry out tasks. . . . This political investment of the body is bound up, in accordance with complex reciprocal relations, with its economic use; it is largely as a force of production that the body is invested with relations of power and domination; but, on the other hand, its constitution as labour power is possible only if it is caught up in a system of subjection . . . ; the body becomes a useful force only if it is both a productive body and a subjected body.[12]

Again, this subjection manifests itself in societal and self-surveillance. Foucault discusses at length the architectural design and psychological implications of an innovative prison model called the Panopticon, which was a tower containing not bars but open windows as well as backlighting, with the goal of officials being able to observe undesirables without their knowing when. (Of course, the prisoners would know that they *might* be under surveillance at any time.) Calling this method of surveillance Panopticism, Foucault observes that "he who is subjected to a field of visibility, and who knows it, assumes responsibilities for the constraints of power; he makes them play spontaneously upon himself; . . . he becomes the principle of his own subjection."[13] Foucault extends this analysis from prison confinement to society at large, charging that similar means to exert control and reinforce confinement can be integrated into virtually any sphere—the military, hospitals, work places. The metaphor of the Panopticon itself, he adds, "has become a transparent building in which the exercise of power may be supervised by society as a whole."[14]

Although in the examples above Foucault focuses on asylums, scientific specialization, and prisons as sources of power, he does not limit such sources to just these three areas. As Foucault asserts in the previous passage, power resides in an amalgam of shape-shifting sources; it cannot be pinpointed to a static "group of institutions and mechanisms that ensure the subservience of the citizens of a given state. . . . It is the moving substrate of force relations," he adds, that "constantly engender states of power" and that are "local and unstable."[15] In other words, power cannot be identified with a sole entity; it is pervasive as well as contingent on which potential source interacts with an individual.

If we accept McElroy's summary of the modern grotesque as the individual's growing powerlessness and subjection to other sources of power, then Foucault's work on power and the surveillance and subjection of the individual can be viewed as a valuable extrapolation of McElroy's description of the social conditions of the modern grotesque, especially as Sherwood Anderson develops the concept by the time he writes *Winesburg, Ohio*. It is in this work where Anderson succeeds in subtly depicting the milieu in which his grotesques grasp onto truths, lead frustrated lives, and seek to communicate their grotesqueness to someone, often George Willard, who will provide understanding. This milieu is in effect a dramatization, a portrait, of the relationship of power, individual subjection, and surveillance as observed by Foucault. Chapter 3 will argue that *Winesburg* can yield many fresh insights if read from a Foucauldian perspective. But a postmodern attention to language can also shed significant light on the book, if we turn our attention to Anderson's deceptively simple prose style.

. . .

As early as 1927, in one of the first biographies of Anderson, Cleveland B. Chase observed that Anderson's prose style had only the illusion of simplicity and was in fact much more complex than it appears at a first glance:

His air of simplicity and ingenuousness, the apparent rambling, the way in which he appears to be haphazardly setting down ideas as they come into his mind in an attempt to discover their meaning, his groping, his artlessness, his naiveté—these are but tricks of the story teller's trade to earn our sympathy for the story which he unfolds graphically and without confusion.[16]

6

Uncovering these "tricks of the story teller's trade" is essential in gaining an understanding of how in his best work Anderson was able to integrate in innovative ways both his subject matter and the manner in which he related that subject matter.

In terms of how he told his tales, Anderson yet again would find himself in good company with postmodern theories, particularly with such theories' concerns with the indeterminate meaning of language. Several years ago David Stouck first detected this tendency in Anderson's work. Finding parallels between Anderson's fiction and the postmodern novel, Stouck noted that "life itself is a fiction, based on a series of temporary arrangements, so that paradoxically the only 'realistic' narrative is one that continually draws the reader's attention to the fact that everything is fictional."[17] What is even more intriguing about Anderson's writing is that if language is always in a state of flux, then he contributes to this instability by means of his purposely evasive narrators. In his best fiction, Anderson deconstructs language without the need of a deconstructionist critic.

Many contemporary theorists of language have argued that with regard to language and objective meaning, never the twain shall meet. As Jacques Derrida had maintained, there is a gulf between the sign and what it signifies—what he called *différance*—that renders meaning to be at best conditional: "The substitution of the sign for the thing itself is both *secondary* and *provisional*: secondary due to an original and lost presence from which the sign thus derives; provisional as concerns this final and missing presence toward which the sign in this sense is a movement of mediation."[18] The "thing itself" cannot manifest a transparent, absolute meaning via language; it remains just outside of language as a "deferred presence." But in order to comprehend this deferred presence, we must realize that *every* sign we use to accomplish this feat is itself "related to something other than itself." Derrida called any such act of interpretation of signs as a "systematic play of differences,"[19] whereby meaning may be deciphered only tentatively, based on the given context of signs. When a public official says she has been "quoted out of context," for example, she is not questioning the accuracy of the actual words quoted but is declaring rather that their meaning has been distorted because they have been isolated from what surrounded them. Derrida used the example of citing a sign as evidence that a sign "can break with every given context, and engender infinitely new contexts in an absolutely nonsaturable fashion. This does not suppose that the mark is valid outside its context, but on the contrary that there are only contexts without any center of absolute anchoring."[20] And as in the case of anything written, the absence of the writer and the immediate, "intended" audience only reinforces the instability of meaning in language.

The hermeneutical theories of Hans Georg Gadamer may contribute some insight into this potential quandary. Gadamer and Derrida may be odd philosophical bedfellows, yet both acknowledge that the meaning of a written text can never be completely grasped.[21] For Gadamer, subjective interpretation is always necessary because the meaning of a text is never transparently clear; in order to interpret a text we have to enter into a "dialogue" with the text as well as with the tradition of previous interpretations. Understanding is tentatively reached when we have entered into a "fusion of horizons" between our present situation and that of the past, culminating in the text itself.[22] As Gadamer describes it: "But the discovery of the true meaning of a text or a work of art is never finished; it is in fact an infinite process. Not only are fresh sources of error constantly excluded, so that all kinds of things are filtered out that obscure the true meaning; but new sources of understanding are continually emerging that reveal unsuspected elements of meaning."[23] With absolute meaning beyond our reach, Gadamer says, the goal of the interpreter is to gain an understanding of what the text says to him. As a result, in entering into a "hermeneutical conversation" with the text and its interpretive tradition,[24] we acquire at best a provisional fixity of meaning, even though we enter into the conversation having a "fore-conception of completeness," an inherent belief that "understanding is likewise guided by the constant transcendent expectations of meaning" that are to be found in the text. Gadamer describes this process as being by necessity open-ended: "All reading involves application, so that a person reading a text is himself part of the meaning he apprehends. . . . The line of meaning that the text manifests to him as he reads it always and necessarily breaks off in an open indeterminacy."[25]

In his conception of a fusion of horizons, Gadamer repeatedly stresses the futility of trying to recover the author's intentions. As he sees it, a work by an author has been left to us, and the text therefore should be the starting point

7

of an interpreter's understanding of it: "The real meaning of a text, as it speaks to the interpreter, does not depend on the contingencies of the author and his original audience." For Gadamer, "texts do not ask to be understood as a living expression of the subjectivity of their writers. This, then, cannot define the limits of a text's meaning."[26] Gadamer may be correct in stressing the interpreter's participation in a text's meaning, but he seems to go too far in discounting the author's role in establishing at least the subject matter of this conversation, via the text the author has written. In other words, an author does not render a final meaning of a text but does, at least, initiate the dialogue between text and interpreter that will yield understanding for subsequent generations of interpreters.

To illustrate this point, in the "Doubloon" chapter of *Moby-Dick*, Melville's narrator presents to the reader a physical description of the Spanish gold coin that Ahab had earlier hammered into the mainmast of the *Pequod*. He then describes a parade, of sorts, as the leading characters approach the doubloon, interpret it, and then move on. Each character invests the coin with a different meaning, usually reflecting that character's personality traits. The cabin boy, Pip, who by this time has gone mad, finally approaches the doubloon and says, "I look, you look, he looks; we look, ye look, they look."[27] Melville's narrator at no point attempts to enlighten the reader of the "true" meaning of the coin; on the contrary, it seems clear that Melville is adamantly undercutting any attempt to assign a fixed, objective meaning, as he does also in the chapter "The Whiteness of the Whale" and elsewhere in the book. Here is a brilliant example of an author establishing the parameters of the interpreter's dialogue with the text, in such a way that the indeterminacy of meaning—not an absolute authorial intention—becomes the starting point of the dialogue.

By the time he writes *Winesburg, Ohio*, Sherwood Anderson would reach a critical moment in his writing career, a moment in which he realized that if characters become grotesques by molding their lives around absolute truths, he as author could not authoritatively describe this process. Hence, the narration in most of the *Winesburg* tales undercuts the "truth" of the storytelling through repeated intrusions by the narrator that destabilize the accuracy and objectivity of the tale he is telling. At the same time, Anderson, through his narrator, demonstrates how language is manipulated, while also contributing to the grotesqueness of his characters. This is one of the main strands of thought throughout this book and will be taken up at greater length in chapter 3, but it is important now to examine the introductory tale in *Winesburg,*

"The Book of the Grotesque," in order to tie together the previous discussion about the modern grotesque and the indeterminacy of language.

.   .   .

In the opening tale of *Winesburg, Ohio,* Anderson seems to provide a concrete definition of the process by which someone becomes a grotesque.[28] *Seems to* is the operative phrase here, because he really provides at best a rough outline of this process. In "The Book of the Grotesque," the narrator describes the old writer's "elaborate theory" of what constitutes grotesqueness: when a person tries to possess a truth and live by it, the truth embraced becomes a falsehood and the person becomes a grotesque.[29] This appears to be a straightforward statement, but we need to unravel a few points: what does Anderson mean by "truth," and why, if he diagnoses the condition of the grotesque, does he not elaborate on a cure?

As the narrator states, "In the beginning when the world was young there were a great many thoughts but no such thing as a truth. Man made the truths himself and each truth was a composite of a great many vague thoughts. All about in the world were the truths and they were all beautiful" (9). In his use of the term *truth,* Anderson implies that a truth is a human construct ("Man made the truths himself") formed as an idealized, abstract concept. Among the "hundreds and hundreds" of truths in the old writer's manuscript, the narrator lists several opposing truths, which touch on passions, material well-being, and personal behavior. Paradoxically, it is when people try to implement these truths that the truths become falsehoods and the people grotesques: "The moment one of the people took one of the truths to himself, called it his truth, and tried to live his life by it, he became a grotesque and the truth he embraced became a falsehood" (9). In other words, people become grotesques when they apply an abstract truth literally to the vicissitudes of everyday living. By grounding these "beautiful" truths into imitable formulas, they are in essence attempting to impose objective meaning onto a very subjective world, which then corrupts the idealized beauty of the truths and traps the individuals into a frustrating and alienating pattern of living.

The narrator lists some of the truths in the old writer's book: "There was the truth of virginity and the truth of passion, the truth of wealth and of poverty, of thrift and of profligacy, of carefulness and abandon" (9). Such truths can only manifest themselves in a social setting, and even though Anderson does not explicitly draw our attention to this point, he implicitly raises several questions. Recalling the earlier discussion of Foucault, we can make several hypotheses about the truths and the grotesques. People do not live in a vacuum, and so society must be the domain in which the truths are snatched up; similarly, if "man" made the truths, then we can assume that truths are prescriptive beliefs created by numerous sources of power in society, and that people "snatch . . . up" one or more of them because they think they will find success and contentment in society by doing so. A tense relationship is thus established between individuals and society at large, whereby the grotesques are inherently assigned responsibility for assuming these truths, even though they may seem to be only unconscious participants in the "long procession of figures." Debate over the causes of grotesqueness and whether the grotesques are responsible for their condition or are merely victims has gone on since the book's first publication.[30] But Judy Jo Small is correct in stating that

> something is amiss when critics try to affix blame for the sufferings of the characters of *Winesburg, Ohio* . . . to any one cause, such as provincialism or puritanical repression or industrialism or capitalism or egotism or patriarchal oppression. . . . A single truth, or a "dozen," will not explain the whole. In keeping with the philosophy it expounds, this tale avoids setting forth any unambiguous "truth."[31]

It is a moot point to single out a sole cause, because not all of the stories that follow the introductory tale will neatly fall under one umbrella cause. It is important to realize both that Anderson depicts his grotesques as characters who respond to a wide spectrum of truths originating from a vast nexus of power sources and that such characters are made to feel responsible for their own embracing of and subjection to these truths.

What Anderson is thus presenting to us in this first tale and throughout *Winesburg* is a manifestation of the modern grotesque. These truths function on a number of levels that lead to the kind of powerlessness and alienation of the individual that McElroy described earlier: they establish a set of normalizing moral codes by which society can watch and judge those who snatch them up; they therefore cause individuals willingly to subject themselves to a set code of acceptable behavior (that is, people convince themselves that they must submit to these codes if they hope to achieve success and contentment in society); and they become as a result unrealistic goals for individuals to attain, setting people up for failure and frustration.

As fleshed out in the other tales of the book, the grotesques are either unable to break free from the particular beliefs they have embraced or forever scarred because they once tried but failed to break free. As we will see in chapter 3, these beliefs run the gamut from those about marital and sexual relations to those about middle-class respectability. Interestingly, we as readers are usually aware of how people became grotesque through the grotesques' attempt to communicate their frustrated lives, as many critics have observed.[32] But here too Anderson compounds the difficulty because his narrator, throughout the book, makes the reader understand that language is an indeterminate source of meaning and is in fact a contributing factor in how individuals become grotesque. He quickly introduces these notions in his introductory tale.

Throughout this story Anderson has his narrator make repeated intrusions that force the reader to question the complete accuracy of the events being described. In explaining the setting in which the old man first conceived of the grotesques, for instance, the narrator tells us about the old man's concerns about his bad health and that "the effect [of such concerns] in fact was quite a special thing and not easily explained" (7). The narrator then attempts to describe how "something inside . . . [the old man] was altogether young" and that this young thing—whether it was a "youth" or a "woman, young, and wearing a coat of mail like a knight"—is what eventually saved him from becoming a grotesque. Admitting frustration, however, the narrator concludes, "It is absurd, you see, to try to tell what was inside the old writer. . . . The thing to get at is what the writer, or the young thing within the writer, was thinking about" (8–9).

Among the "great many notions in his head," the narrator tells us, was the old man's unique knowledge of all the people he had met; for he had "known them in a peculiarly intimate way that was different from the way in which you . . . know people" (8). Again sensing frustration with his inadequacy in relating the tale, the narrator asks us, "Why quarrel with an old man concerning his thoughts?" In these first few paragraphs of the story, Anderson is purposely obfuscating a clear-cut meaning by having his narrator admit that words are inadequate and can at best provide only an approximate or tentative meaning. This overt tentativeness continues in the key passages of the tale in which the narrator attempts to describe the old man's "elaborate theory" as set down in his unpublished manuscript, "The Book of the Grotesque."

The narrator leads up to this description by informing the reader of the effect the old man's book had on him when he says, "I saw it once and it made

11

an indelible impression on my mind. The book had one central thought that is very strange and has always remained with me. By remembering it I have been able to understand many people and things that I was never able to understand before. *The thought was involved but a simple statement of it would be something like this . . .*" (9, emphasis mine). Despite the profound influence he says the book had on him, the narrator only provides the reader with a "simple statement" of the old man's theory. What had seemed so definitive on a first glance the narrator admits to being only a rough outline. Also, its influence allowed him not to know many people and things better but to understand them better. Note the emphasized ambiguity: knowing implies a definitive grasp of something factual, while understanding implies a more intuitive grasp of something that is nonetheless comprehensive. This is an important distinction that will gain in significance by the climax of the book in "Sophistication," where Anderson will provide enough clues to suggest that a "cure" to grotesqueness can be found.

The old man, "who had spent all his life writing and was filled with words" (9), composes his manuscript about the grotesques but never publishes it. The narrator, meanwhile, can only provide a "simple statement" of the old man's theory of the grotesques and in recounting the tale gives the reader at best a provisional approximation of its "true" meaning. Anderson thus cleverly sets a stage whereon his readers must complete the tale for both the characters and for themselves. In this and in most of the other stories in the book, Anderson successfully avoids preaching pat, absolute answers to the dilemma of the modern grotesque. Had he done so, he would have ironically fallen victim to his own rough definition of the grotesque.[33]

Before we delve into the rest of the book, we need to reexamine Anderson's first two published novels, *Windy McPherson's Son* (1916) and *Marching Men* (1917), as well as the unpublished *Talbot Whittingham* (written just before he commenced writing the *Winesburg* stories), to trace the evolution of Anderson's conceptualization of the modern grotesque. These works, after all, extend the "fusion of horizons" for our understanding of *Winesburg*. In other words, these early works comprise a thematic foundation on which Anderson will construct his *Winesburg* tales. In these earlier works we will see how Anderson rather clumsily attempts to diagnose the ills of modern society and prescribe definitive cures for them. But in these works we can also discern the rough seeds that will blossom into *Winesburg*. Applying postmodern theories of power relations and language will aid us in this discernment.

CHAPTER TWO

The Early Novels

ESTABLISHING THE HORIZON
FOR *WINESBURG*

> Having listened to talk and having myself talked overmuch, I
> grow weary of talk and walk in the streets.[1]

In *Winesburg, Ohio,* Sherwood Anderson successfully combined an original concept of the modern grotesque with an innovative understanding of the indeterminacy of language. But he did not forge these ideas out of whole cloth; in particular, his perceptive attention to the alienation of modern Americans and their inability to communicate can be traced back to his first attempts at writing fiction. When he began such writing in about 1908 he had garnered many of the material trophies that signified success in mainstream America: a powerful position as his own boss in a manufacturing company; a marriage to a woman from the prominent social circles of Cleveland; the beginnings of a family; and respected social standing in the community. In the midst of his growing prosperity, however, Anderson began to question the cultural icons of middle-class respectability, and he explored these concerns in his fiction. By the time he left his family and job in Ohio to go to Chicago in early 1913 he was already quite familiar with identifying what he perceived to be a negative transformation taking place in modern society. He was still quite inexperienced, though, in adopting a language and a style suitable for critiquing this transformation.

Three months after his soon-to-be mythologized mental breakdown in Elyria, Ohio, in November of 1912, Sherwood Anderson left his wife and children and settled in Chicago, where he got work writing for an advertising agency. He brought with him several novel-length manuscripts, two of which would eventually see publication as *Windy McPherson's Son* (1916) and *Marching Men* (1917).[2] In these novels, as well as in the unpublished *Talbot Whittingham*, we can see Anderson groping toward the kind of mastery over his material and the confidence in his writing he would eventually achieve in *Winesburg*. By themselves, these works are the crude, often bizarre attempts of an author trying to depict the social ills of the early twentieth century and plainly working out on paper his slowly evolving thought. At the same time that he is trying to articulate these innovative thoughts, however, he allows himself to organize and write them down according to the fashions of popular-fiction writers. It is not a happy marriage. According to Harry Hansen, Anderson himself said of his early works, "The books frankly were not good."[3]

All three works focus on the maturation of a sensitive youth who, in his adulthood, comes to recognize the shallowness and spiritual hollowness of modern mainstream America. The matured youth then self-consciously attempts to find meaning in an apparently meaningless world and become a model, or actual leader, for the rest of humanity, which suffers from perpetual ennui. Invariably, however, the stories devolve into quasi-philosophical quests having no viable conclusions. In each work, the defeated mass of humanity is viewed from the point of view of our self-conscious heroes. Throughout each work the narrator is constantly interceding for these heroes, telling us about the ills of society and validating their quests for truth (*Windy McPherson's Son*) or order and form (*Marching Men*) or beauty (*Talbot Whittingham*).

Simply stated, all three works are failures, in part because Anderson seems fixated on unrealistically elevating his protagonists to the level of Emersonian Great Men or Nietzschean Supermen who are hell-bent on curing society's ills. He describes the frustrations of modern life realistically while at the same time giving us fairy-tale heroes. In addition, not yet aware of the power of language, he employs a heavy-handed, didactic approach in telling his stories. Ironically, in light of the insights he would invoke in "The Book of the Grotesque," each protagonist of these early novels would be deemed a grotesque.

These works are fascinating to examine nonetheless, because they extend our "fusion of horizons" for *Winesburg*. In these three early novels Anderson confronts issues that will become the basis of his conception of the modern grotesque. The novels are innovative in snatches: they begin to explore critically the negative consequences on the individual of the normalized, controlling power sources that would characterize modern industrialized America, and as such, they exemplify in traces some of Foucault's observations on the subjection of the individual. But in contrast to *Winesburg,* these works display at best scant signs of the kind of innovative experimentation in language that distinguishes *Winesburg* as a precursor to postmodernist fiction. As we will see, the *material* of the modern grotesque is present in these works; but it is not successfully integrated with the *telling* of it.

.   .   :

Windy McPherson's Son opens in Caxton, Iowa, where Sam McPherson, a young teenager who sells newspapers, is regarded as "a figure in the town's life" because of his industriousness and cleverness.[4] At this early age, Sam already has an understanding of many of the power sources that affect his life. His father Windy is a loquacious alcoholic who continually causes embarrassment in Sam's life. Though Sam is accepted by the town and is a regular fixture among a coterie of townsmen who loaf and talk at Wildman's grocery, he nevertheless feels compelled to assert his business prowess as a way to compensate for being "Windy McPherson's son." No one ever taunts Sam about his father, but he still forms his work ethic around proving to the town that he is not another Windy:

> The realisation of the fact that his father was a confirmed liar and braggart had for years cast a shadow over his days and the shadow had been made blacker by the fact that in a land where the least fortunate can laugh in the face of want he had more than once stood face to face with poverty. He believed that the logical answer to the situation was money in the bank and with all the ardour of his boy's heart he strove to realise that answer. He wanted to be a money-maker and the totals at the foot of the pages in the soiled yellow bankbook were the milestones that marked the progress he had already made. They told him that the daily struggles . . . were not without fruit. (22)

This passage ably illustrates some of the most important influences on Sam's life. Personally embarrassed by his father's wayward behavior, Sam is also well aware of the power of town gossip, as well as of the pervasive hold that the American Dream myth had on Americans in both great cities and small towns like Caxton. He not only constantly tries to manifest an autonomous self-reliance, he also convinces himself of the importance of exerting mastery over others, to be in command not only of himself but of everyone he encounters.

15

Not surprisingly, at age fifteen "the call of the city came to him" (74); his growing obsession with domination becomes too great for the little corn town. Ironically, though, Sam's hunger for power and control shows him to be the agent of his own subjection to the then-prevailing ideology of "getting up in the world." Later in the novel, when Sam becomes a ruthless business tycoon in Chicago, the narrator tells us that from that point on, Sam's story "ceases to be the story of a man and becomes the story of a type" (248). But, really, Sam chooses to be a type before he leaves the Caxton city limits. In a Foucauldian sense, he assumes responsibility for his own subjection by acting on powerful cultural myths and gauging his actions by how others may judge him.

The town repeatedly reinforces Sam's work ethic. Valmore, one of the cohorts who regularly gather at the grocery, admits that "it is money makes the mare go" (75). Such bromides as this fill "the very air [Sam] breathed" and feed the "belief within him that to make money and to have money would in some way make up for the old half-forgotten humiliations in the life of the McPherson family" (74). With this fixed goal in mind, Sam quickly determines what will help him succeed and what will not.

Religion and thoughts about God will not help him, for reasons that intersect each of the major influences on him: his father, town gossip, and his belief in the success myth. He perceives religion and God to be embarrassing and counterproductive to his goal of being a powerful businessman. In a brief moment of piety, he takes to reading the Bible in secret, even hiding it under his pillow whenever his mother appears near his room: "He thought it something not quite in keeping with his aims as a business man and a money getter to be concerned about his soul" (39). Regularly in tow with his mother at church services, he usually fills the time by sleeping. When the minister talks to him about this, Sam finds it repulsive and immediately associates the minister and his message with both the sleepy town and his lying father: "He thought himself superior to the thin-lipped man . . . and had he been able to express what was in his heart he might have said, 'Look here, man! I am made of different stuff from all the people there at the church. I am new clay to be moulded into a new man. . . . I do not accept your ideas of life any more than I accept Windy McPherson just because he happens to be my father'" (39). What finalizes his break with religion at this period in his life is his humiliation at a religious revival, where he convinces himself that organized religion is primarily a means of converting the townsfolk into mindless subjects. At the revival, the minister calls on the congregation to stand up and give testimony to Jesus; everyone complies except Sam, who tries to hide behind his mother. But when he is singled out to testify, Sam embarrasses himself by garbling a line of scripture as his response. The congregation laughs at him, and Sam storms out, angered and ashamed that his actions will end up an object of ridicule in all the town gossip. Alienated by his bungled public display of piety, Sam is convinced that church "is a place to make public asses of the people" (45).

Sex, or as Anderson calls it, "the sex motive" (41), is another hindrance. Sam's mentor, the self-professed dandy John Telfer, repeatedly attempts to set Sam straight concerning women. He tells Sam that women "are not the real things. . . . I would have you observe women's minds and avoid letting them influence your own. . . . They live in a world of unrealities" (60). He persuades Sam that women function as distractions to a man of genius, whom he believes Sam to be, when he says, "I think that a man or boy who has set for himself a task had better let women and girls alone" (69). What is really at issue, though, is that "the sex motive" is something that Sam cannot readily control; hence, it remains mysterious, sometimes even dangerous, to him. As J. R. Scafidel points out, Sam eventually tries to exert control over sex in his adult years, with frustrated results: "He feels he must order this force of sex, as man has nature, so he sublimates it."[5] This imposing of order on sex becomes more obvious when Sam codifies his sexual relations with Sue Rainey in their self-conscious mission to serve "mankind through children" (188). Even though he displays a normal teenage curiosity about sex, he nonetheless subjects himself to the misogynistic views of Telfer, as when he tells himself, "I will try to be a man. I will try to not have anything to do with them—with women. I will work and make money—and—and—" (73). Sam again shows himself to be malleable to the influences of the town, in this case, to advance his career in business.

A cruder manifestation of the town's influence is the widespread power of gossiping. For instance, Anderson contrasts Sam's humiliation at church with the arrest of Mike McCarthy, the village atheist, who is apprehended for killing a man because of his involvement with the man's wife. In an apparent state of madness, McCarthy, while in jail and with the townsfolk milling about outside, delivers a prayer that all can hear: he curses the "sons of this cesspool of respectability" and identifies a dozen wives with whom he claims to have had affairs. From this outburst, Sam gains an "ugly feeling of satisfaction" because some of the women named were a moment earlier such seemingly pious participants in the revival.

17

Another example of the pernicious influence of town gossip is Mary Under-wood, a schoolteacher of Sam's, who leads an isolated, ostracized life:

> Mary did not understand the people of Caxton and the people misunder-stood and distrusted her. Taking no part in the life of the town and keeping to herself and to her books she awoke a kind of fear in others. Because she did not join them at church suppers, or go from porch to porch gossiping with other women through the long summer evenings, they thought her something abnormal. (57)

A controversial incident involving Mary and her school results in gossip about the incident making the rounds in town. Sam, however, sees through the gossip and associates it with his father's penchant for telling lies (59). Mary is again thrust into the town's limelight at the funeral of Jane McPherson, Sam's mother, because she appeared at the McPherson house one night during the mother's illness. Sam goes so far as to attack in public two women who were discussing Mary; their gossiping prompts a lengthy authorial diatribe on the evils of women who gossip. Sam then publishes a letter in the local newspaper defending Mary, and soon after heads to Chicago to begin his journey to success.

In the first book, the most effective part of the novel, Anderson presents a compelling depiction of someone who wills his own subjection by playing a role, the characteristics of which have been fashioned by various sources of power. Convinced that he must become a superior person in order to offset the town's surveillance of the McPherson family, Sam is ever on the alert to expand his business prowess, even if that means subjugating his sexual de-sires. Paradoxically, at the same time that he tries to project himself to the town as a budding genius in business, he loathes the town for its shallow mindedness and its widespread control of its inhabitants, as demonstrated by the effects of its gossiping on characters like Mary Underwood. As in Foucault's interpretation of the Panopticon, the town serves as a place where individu-als' actions stand out in relief so that they can be watched and evaluated for how well they serve or deviate from normalized morality. Characters who are uniquely individualized (and praised for it by the narrator's spokesman John Telfer) are regarded askance by the town. Sam does not suffer such ostracism because he embraces the work ethic that was then revered in the nation's popu-lar mythology. Having subjected himself to playing out his self-assigned role, Sam is, in a sense, complicit in sustaining the ideological status quo. He differs primarily in his motivation to succeed; his distaste for the town's lies is merely a projection of his hatred for his lying father, and thus it is this desire to distance himself from lies and embarrassments that propels him to reject Caxton and stake his claim in Chicago.

In the chapters following book 1, Anderson tries his best to excoriate the crushing power of the modern business work ethic on the individual and to find definitive answers to this problem, but his ineptitude in conveying his ideas undercuts the overall effectiveness of the novel. In having Sam eventually become a searcher of Truth, Anderson undermines his depiction of the ills of modern life as he molds Sam into a rather grotesque figure.

Early on in Chicago, Sam envisions himself becoming a self-made man, an achiever of the rags-to-riches version of the American Dream. Still desiring to distinguish himself from his father and the small minds of Caxton, he yearns to wield power over men: "He saw himself going on and on, directing, managing, ruling men. It seemed to him that there was nothing he could not do. 'I will run factories and banks and maybe mines and railroads,' he thought" (138). At twenty-two Sam already has begun to rise up in the Rainey Arms Company, becoming an efficiency expert and preparing himself for his eventual takeover of the company. In the course of only a few years, he and his cohorts become known as the "McPherson Chicago crowd" (249) for their boldness in controlling a variety of industries. Clearly ignorant of big business, Anderson, in the sections devoted to Sam's rise to power, resorts to clichéd images of business dealings to hurry along his protagonist's growing material success. He is clearly trying hard to prepare his readers for Sam's dramatic rejection of the American Dream to pursue Truth, a pursuit that is spurred on after he and his wife, Sue Rainey, split and his father-in-law, Colonel Tom, commits suicide as a result of Sam's takeover of the arms company. Anderson, intending to shock, describes Sam's rejection of material success: "He, an American multi-millionaire, a man in the midst of his money-making, one who had realised the American dream, to have sickened at the feast . . . —to seek Truth, to seek God" (258). But Anderson deludes himself and his readers into thinking that at this moment Sam becomes a truth seeker; for throughout much of the novel Sam has tried to live according to the prescriptive "truths" of the American Dream, and, in his courtship of and marriage to Sue Rainey, he (and apparently the author) is fascinated with shaping his life around a single truth as an antidote to modern existence. Ironically, these traits will a few years later become for Anderson characteristics of grotesqueness.

19

When Sam proposes marriage to Sue, she quizzes him to make sure he is "ready to believe what [she] believe[s] and to live for what [she] want[s] to live" (186). "Her idea was one of service to mankind through children," the narrator tells us, adding, "She had thought it all out . . . and wanted a husband in accord with her ideas" (188). Sam soon agrees: "He had completely and wholly accepted Sue's conception of life" (201). Thus begins a period in Sam's life that is marked by continual frustration, because three attempts to conceive a child result in miscarriages or stillbirths. The two are simply stymied over their failure to have children, and they both feel that their marriage is now without purpose. After all, Sam had confused the love of his wife with a love of her ideas, and he had even set aside his quest to be a great business-man, all to pursue those ideas: "He was a man with children in his loins and he had given up his struggles for business eminence for the sake of preparing himself for a kind of noble fatherhood of children, many children, strong children" (222).

For the rest of the book, Sam pursues one single truth after another, with a ludicrous procession of starts and restarts. After he decides that serving humankind through children is unattainable, he vows to "take hold anew and work out for [himself] a programme for a way of life" (225). Sue meanwhile decides to pursue activities for "the great modern movement of social uplift," a pursuit that becomes a series of exercises in parlor socialism. Sam returns to hard-hearted business practices and, on the verge of acquiring the arms company, realizes that "the best men spend their lives seeking truth" (240). With this line as his mantra, soon afterward he sets out on a vagabond life, dabbling in various activities from social reforms to bartending. The story has long unraveled by this time, as we are led from one escapade to another, all dictated by Sam's near-desperate desire to find a definitive way to lead his life: "He had one principle of action; whenever an idea came into his mind he did not hesitate, but began trying at once the practicability of living by following the idea" (287). Running out of ideas for him to pursue, Anderson eventually has Sam purchase three children from an uncaring mother and return home to Sue, who takes them all in.[6]

Having successfully sketched the various forms of societal control and critiqued how someone becomes subjected to the standardized morality and mores of society, Anderson fails overall to create a cohesive and effective tale in which to portray these issues. Much of the reason stems from Anderson's inexperience at writing fiction and thus his having been influenced by what he thought should appear in serious novels. As Anderson observed about the book: "At the time the book was written, circumstances and a false conception of what is due the reader of a novel led me into something like trickery in writing. . . . I am afraid I had come to novel writing from novel reading. I could not leave Sam in my reader's hands having achieved nothing but money and weariness."[7] Choosing to depict Sam as a heroic truth seeker, Anderson paints himself into a corner. Not wanting to have his protagonist, who rejects the materialistic strains of the American Dream, seem a failure as measured by conventional standards, a failure that might have caused conventional readers to question Anderson's criticisms, he felt compelled to show his audience that Sam "makes good" after all.

Throughout the book Anderson seems fascinated with those who exert power and control, even occasionally defending the robber barons of his own youth.[8] In this and in his other early fiction before *Winesburg,* Anderson seems to prefer siding with heroic figures who emerge from the dross of society. The mass of humanity has not yet elicited Anderson's sympathies as it would by the time he writes *Winesburg.*

In *Windy McPherson's Son,* Anderson only occasionally displays the kind of concern for the down-and-out that will become his focal point in *Winesburg.* His depiction of Sam's mother, Jane, is one exception, as is the brief glimpse he gives us of a prostitute Sam encounters during his vagabond period. In this example, he uses language that will evolve in his subsequent early novels: "She had . . . a look of hard chastity, like one whipped but not defeated" (319). Even Janet Eberly, a physical cripple but intellectual dynamo for Sam, is given fleeting treatment before she dies, although Sam "thought of her as in a sense his wife" (159). The strong-willed but crippled milliner yields to the strong-willed but healthy and wealthy Sue Rainey.

Intertwined with Sam's heroic quests are the author's own, as several passages about art and the artist illustrate; in these the Nietzschean overtones are hard to miss. Early in the book, Telfer rhapsodizes about the true artist, and his musings correspond with Sam's desire for power and Truth: "An artist is one who hungers and thirsts after perfection. . . . It is the artist who, among all men, has the divine audacity. Does he not hurl himself into a battle in which is engaged against him all of the accumulative genius of the world?" (13). Later, again with a mind on the artist, Telfer tells Sam, "The world will some day grope its way into some kind of an understanding of its extraordinary men. Now they suffer terribly. . . . It is only the common, the plain, unthinking man who slides

21

peacefully through this troubled world" (55). In this book, the "common man" remains out of focus for Anderson; his preference is a societal and artistic Superman, as the narrator equates the two when Sam is making his mark in Chicago: "The stroke that he saw in the hand of the successful business men about him is the stroke also of the master painter, scientist, actor, singer, prize fighter" (121). These quasi-Nietzschean preoccupations will grow in intensity over Anderson's next two novels, as he will again have more success in diagnosing modern social ills than in providing any cures. But he will also begin to turn his attention to those figures who will evolve into the grotesques.

. . .

With *Marching Men* (1917), published a year after *Windy McPherson's Son*, Anderson revisits the milieu of the modern grotesque: the powerlessness of the individual, the sharp disparity between ordinary workers and those who wield control over them, and the paradox of individuals subjected to forces of power, yet sharing some responsibility for their subjection. But with this book Anderson also shows early signs of understanding the inefficacy of language that he would explore more rewardingly in *Winesburg, Ohio;* in addition, he develops at greater length than in his first book the concept of what will evolve into the grotesques.

In spite of these positive developments in Anderson's second novel, there remain deficiencies that mar these achievements, such as his continued preoccupation with Nietzschean exemplary men, rather than the downtrodden, and his repeated fixation with serving up definitive answers to the problems of modern American society. In many ways, particularly in those stemming from the novel's basic premise, *Marching Men* is less of a book than its predecessor. But Anderson's heightened awareness of language alone makes this novel worthy of consideration, as a precursor to *Winesburg*.

With Norman McGregor, a disgruntled youth in Coal Creek, Pennsylvania, Anderson presents us with a character who is thoroughly fascinated with power as a means of exerting mastery over others—a power that for much of the book is directed against ordinary people. Unlike Sam McPherson, McGregor does not look to the myth of the American Dream as a way of validating his identity; in fact, using brute force against society is McGregor's primary mode of asserting his identity. Working against the rags-to-riches model he used in his first book, Anderson here keeps his protagonist situated on the margins of society, both in his hometown and in the big city. While a boy in Coal Creek,

McGregor realizes he is different from his fellow townsfolk and directs his pent-up anger toward those in his immediate society. In the novel's first book, we see him constantly pitting himself against the town because he has not yet understood the importance of situating the town within the larger societal context, an understanding that would allow him to at least sympathize with the powerlessness of his peers. Instead, he is actually complicit with the larger power forces of society, about which he is, at this point, ignorant.

Within the first two pages of the novel we are given one clue as to why Norman McGregor has such contempt for his peers and remains separate from them. As a lark, McGregor's uncle decides to rename his nephew Beaut because of Norman's rough physical features. This act echoes his father's having been nicknamed "Cracked" McGregor because of his perceived difference from his fellow townsmen. From here and for the rest of the first book the narrator provides numerous instances in which McGregor expresses hatred for the town, often speaking sympathetically on his behalf, as he does here: "The country is like a vast disorganised undisciplined army, leaderless, uninspired, going in route-step along the road to they know not what end."9

The cause of this widespread inertia seems to be twofold, according to Anderson. On the one hand there are the power forces that own the mines, where virtually everyone works, as well as the houses and stores in the town. As the narrator explains, "In the town men lived like brutes. Dumb with toil they drank greedily in the saloon on Main Street and went home to beat their wives. Among them a constant low muttering went on. They felt the injustice of their lot but could not voice it logically" (39). On the other hand, the workers accept the status quo. In the first book, McGregor finds himself set apart from his peers because he recognizes, as they do not, that the workers are mostly to blame for their condition. Unable to "voice [the injustice] logically," McGregor turns to physical force as the only means of jarring the workers' passivity. In this first section of the novel, Anderson, as well as his protagonist, would seem to share Foucault's views on individuals being the source of their powerlessness.

In another early scene McGregor and a fellow outcast are perched on a hillside overlooking the town. When McGregor asks him what he would do to the town if he had the power, the youth tells him, "I would go among men like Christ.... Poor and humble, I would go teaching them of love" (52). Rejecting this benevolent Christian approach, McGregor launches into a Nietzschean sermon to the town that accentuates his preference for action over words:

23

> Men of Coal Creek, . . . listen to the voice of McGregor. I hate you. I hate
> you because you jeered at my father and at me and because you cheated
> my mother, Nance McGregor. I hate you because, you are weak and
> disorganised like cattle. I would like to come along and teach you the power
> of force. I would like to slay you one by one, not with weapons but with my
> naked fists. (52–53)

One might wonder at this point why Anderson dedicated the book to "Ameri-can Workingmen" when he and his protagonist have such a seething disdain for them. But this scene underscores the potentially radical, though incho-ately conceived, message of the book. Prefiguring a similar debate (Christ vs. Nietzsche) that will be more developed in *Talbot Whittingham,* this passage illustrates Anderson's own frustration over the seeming powerlessness of the masses, their inertia perpetuated by small-minded acts of meanness, their potential force against the larger power structures in society displaced. To the narrator, as well as his protagonist, American workers who remain unfocused and disorganized deserve their fate, as McGregor confirms in this same pas-sage: "If they have made you work like rats buried in a hole they are right" (53). Thinking their situation hopeless, McGregor would rather mow them all down than rouse them into action. He is a Superman-in-waiting, but at this point in the book he vents his angry feelings only toward those who are im-mediately around him, men who deem him and his father as "cracked" and who destroyed his mother's grocery store during a strike.

It is not surprising, then, that during this same strike McGregor displays great sympathy for a detachment of soldiers who were sent to break up the job action: "His blood was stirred by the sight of them marching shoulder to shoulder. He thought there was order and decency in the rank of uniformed men moving silently and quickly along and he half wished they would de-stroy the town" (40–41). Ironically, McGregor is drawn to the rank and file of faceless soldiers who, in the larger context of the book, represent the forces that perpetuate the suppression of the workers. He has little faith in the fickleness of individuals and instead admires this body of men who are uni-formly devoid of individual characteristics. Like Sam McPherson, McGregor is relieved to leave the town and settle in Chicago. But it is only when he returns to Coal Creek to attend his mother's funeral that he begins to sympa-thize and understand the plight of American workers and eventually to focus his energy on using his growing powers for them rather than against them.

When he first enters Chicago, McGregor is uncertain about his future prospects; he was, after all, simply relieved to have left behind the "pygmies" of Coal Creek. He is determined, however, to assert mastery over humankind in some tangible way as a means of validating his identity: "In Chicago he meant to do something. Coming from a community where no man arose above a condition of silent brute labour he meant to step up into the light of power. Filled with hatred and contempt of mankind he meant that mankind should serve him" (63). He soon realizes, though, that the disorder and decay of Coal Creek are to be found also in Chicago. Regarding life in the city, McGregor muses, "There is still going on the attempt to force me into the hole in the ground. There is a hole here in which men live and work just as there is in the mining town from which I came" (127). Even though he advances to the position of foreman in an apple warehouse within a few years, he remains dissatisfied and uninterested in traditional notions of rising in the world, because he realizes that this "dreary dream" results not in order but in slovenliness (101). Until his mother's death brings him back home, he remains unfocused and frustrated: "He was striving to get a hold of some elusive quality in life that seemed to be forever out of reach" (106). Again, he automatically associates this unsettling desire with physical action: "The desire in McGregor for some kind of activity became a madness. His body shook with the strength of his desire to end the vast disorder of life" (107–8).

During his mother's funeral, the miners follow the hearse on the way to the cemetery. Suddenly, their stooped shoulders become erect, and they begin to march in unison, a change that McGregor notices. It is an epiphanic moment for him:

> In a flash he knew that he who had hated the miners hated them no more. With Napoleonic insight he read a lesson into the accident of the men's falling into step behind his carriage. A big grim thought flashed into his brain. "Some day a man will come who will swing all of the workers of the world into step like that. . . . He will make them conquer, not one another but the terrifying disorder of life. If their lives have been wrecked by disorder it is not their fault. They have been betrayed by the ambitions of their leaders, all men have betrayed them." (148–49)

McGregor begins to see the plight of the workers in the larger context of societal power relations. Being a man of force and action, he deems them children in need of leadership: "They are children. . . . Suppose they could just learn to march, nothing else. Suppose they should begin to do with their bodies what their minds are not strong enough to do" (149). Understanding at last their inability to give active expression of themselves, McGregor realizes that he might become a strong leader who will speak for them in some meaningful way.

Back in Chicago, groping toward some means of providing such leadership, McGregor more clearly articulates his dissatisfaction with the so-called sophisticated urban life. Speaking for him, the narrator describes those who are trying to rise up in the world as suffering a kind of inertia similar to that of the workers in Coal Creek. Calling it the "disease of comfort and prosperity" (158), he characterizes the contented, comfortable middle classes—as well as those who aspire to them—as being "mere slaves to words and formulas" (124). In one scene, before Nance McGregor's funeral, the narrator contrasts McGregor with his fellow Chicagoans and states that what distinguishes McGregor from the rest of the pack is his awareness that aping the thoughts and words of everyone else makes one a "mere toiling, food-consuming chattering puppet to the gods" (123). Such inquiries as this one into the manipulation of language mark a significant feature in the novel, one that generally has been overlooked by critics and that demonstrates a growing and maturing sense of consciousness in Anderson about language and meaning and their manipulation. This newfound attention to language is the novel's saving grace, because it displays a postmodern sensibility that Anderson will develop more successfully in *Winesburg*.

Anderson begins to pinpoint McGregor's impatience and frustration with the masses in McGregor's realization that when language becomes affixed with a concrete meaning, it produces a blind passivity in individuals of a kind that facilitates their being controlled and subjugated. In the passage just quoted, the narrator elaborates on the contrast between McGregor and his peers: "For the others life let itself run out in the endless doing of little tasks, the thinking of little thoughts and the saying of groups of words over and over endlessly like parrots that sit in cages and earn their bread by screaming two or three sentences to passers by" (122–23).

Such "slaves to words and formulas" have an uncanny resemblance to the grotesques of *Winesburg*, who pattern their lives according to formulaic truths and make frustrated attempts to move beyond their condition. In fact, one scene could stand as an early version of the old man's dream in "The Book of the Grotesque": McGregor one night leaves a saloon, feeling overwhelmed by the task he has set for himself. He suddenly takes note of the crowds passing by him and sees them as a long train of defeated individuals:

> The pitiful insignificance of the individual was apparent. As in a long procession the figures of the individuals who had tried to rise out of the ruck of American life passed before him. With a shudder he realised that for the most part the men whose names filled the pages of American history meant nothing. . . . Like the men passing in the street they went across the face of things and disappeared into the darkness. (217)

The "procession of figures" is akin to the line of individuals who each appear in the old man's dream to snatch up one or more of the truths (*Winesburg* 9). McGregor's peers in the Chicago streets, like the grotesques, pass across "the face of things" and disappear into virtual nothingness. And like the grotesques, the individuals in *Marching Men* have sanctioned their insignificance by submitting themselves to accepted formulas and then allowing themselves to be judged by various sources in society. The manipulation of language is a key force in both the grotesqueness of the *Winesburg* characters and the insignificance of the *Marching Men* masses.

McGregor's distrust of language reinforces his fondness for action, because action at least seems to produce tangible, real results, while language and its manipulation result in deception. As McGregor thinks to himself,

> Words mean nothing but when a man marches with a thousand other men and is not doing it for the glory of some king, then it will mean something. He will know then that he is a part of something real and he will catch the rhythm of the mass and glory in the fact that he is a part of the mass and that the mass has meaning. He will begin to feel great and powerful. (150–51)

For McGregor, words act only as a means of negating action, since they are used to captivate listeners and keep them in check, which results in the preservation of the status quo. For example, while he is taking night classes, McGregor has an argument with his professor, who had been casually speaking to his class about world unrest. He tells the instructor, "We go from room to room hearing talk. . . . On the street corners downtown in the evenings and in towns and villages men talk and talk. Books are written, jaws wag. The jaws of men are loose. They wabble about—saying nothing. . . . If there is all this unrest why does it not

27

come to something?" (167). The failure of language to inspire action explains why McGregor initially fails to inaugurate his plan for the Marching Men: "For years McGregor tried to get it under way by talking. He did not succeed" (247).

Once his venture finally gets off the ground, it quickly gains attention—in part because McGregor commands that his marching workers remain silent: "Be silent. . . . That's the best thing to do. Be silent and attend to business and your marching will be ten times more effective" (249). By not confining the movement's purpose to a conventionalized platform of ideas and grievances, McGregor creates for the public something of a vacuum, for people cannot readily assign meaning to the movement without having any linguistic markers with which to compare it (such as "socialism," a concept for which McGregor has nothing but disdain anyway). When a reporter asks McGregor what the movement is about, he tells him, "It's creeping in among them. . . . The thing that can't be put into words is getting itself expressed. . . . A new force is coming into the world" (252–53). He elaborates, "For a time men will cease to be individuals. They will become a mass, a moving all-powerful mass. They will not put their thoughts into words but nevertheless there will be a thought growing up in them" (253). With language being corrupted, tangible meaning can only be derived from nonlinguistic sources. (This will be a key insight developed further in *Winesburg*.) In this same scene, as if illustrating his point, McGregor confronts a marching worker who is complaining of sore feet, pummels him, and then explains, "This is no time for words. . . . This is not a game. It's the beginning of men's realisation of themselves. Get in there and say nothing" (256). Later we are told that McGregor reaches his audiences not by confusing them with great oratory but by drawing "for them great scrawling pictures" (295). No doubt slugging a straggling marcher drew a clearer picture than his subsequent explanation.

In *Marching Men* Anderson makes significant advances in developing his portrait of the modern grotesque, particularly by his insightful treatment of the power of language. But as this last scene illustrates, he still has to evolve considerably both as a storyteller and as a critic of modern America. The work therefore remains seriously flawed for a number of reasons.

Most important, Anderson's preoccupation with creating a Superman who can exert mastery over others, as well as his prescription of silent marching as an antidote to individual powerlessness, is as formulaic as people's enslavement to words. Ironically, his cure for this powerlessness is just another form of subjection: people must surrender their individuality in marching as a mass, trusting that their Nietzschean leader represents their collective interests. As John Ditsky has correctly observed, McGregor becomes "the sort of single-idea grotesque that is the substance of *Winesburg*."[10] Furthermore, McGregor may indeed have an understanding of the downtrodden masses, but throughout the book he is completely aloof from virtually every person he encounters, making him a rather isolated leader. Countless times while he is in Chicago, for example, McGregor walks through the streets while brooding over his plans; rarely does he ever take note of the people he passes. Clarence B. Lindsay has commented on what he calls McGregor and Sam McPherson's "disengagement" with their surroundings, arguing that "Beaut . . . [is] too preoccupied to experience what . . . [he is] moving through. . . . In Beaut's case, ironically he is often so preoccupied with the issue of disorder, his plans for his peculiar marching, that he can't see the city which supposedly is the very condition which demands order."[11]

This disengagement can be seen also in McGregor's dealings with specific individuals such as Edith Carson, whom McGregor finally chooses over the wealthy and beautiful Margaret Ormsby. For two years McGregor is a regular visitor to Carson's apartment, where inevitably he spends the time talking about himself and his life in Coal Creek. In one scene he even visits Carson to "think out the matter of marrying Margaret Ormsby" (232). The several scenes involving his interactions with Carson and Ormsby, including McGregor's internal debates over a new kind of woman being needed, end up functioning as a tired refrain that appeared in Anderson's first book and would often reappear in his subsequent works.

In addition, as he did in *Windy McPherson's Son*, Anderson hashes out a pet theory that has the role of the artist enveloped within a Nietzschean mantle, again with the result that his own personal interest in elevating the artist detracts from his storytelling. He does work out a tortured syllogism in which he allies the artist's "passion for form" (66) with the fact that only "masters of human life have understood" this passion (84–85) and that, therefore, McGregor is a "crude kind of artist" (284); but as he also did in his first book, in which Sam is an artist type, Anderson unconvincingly equates his heroic protagonists and the artist. (In sharp contrast, in *Winesburg* he will have his narrator make, at the most, veiled references about the role of the artist or poet, but there he will do so for more substantive reasons.)

Missing in *Marching Men* is the kind of attention Anderson pays to the downtrodden masses in greater depth in *Winesburg*. The closest we get to an intimate portrait of such characters is the brief treatment of Edith Carson, the lonely milliner whose silent perseverance culminates in a passionate defense of herself while in front of Margaret Ormsby as a marriage prospect for McGregor. But really, there are no other characters like her, except for the faceless masses or the caricatures of the wealthy that otherwise pervade the book. Anderson will become more conscious of the defeated lives of individuals, though still in an abstracted way, in his next work, *Talbot Whittingham*, a book that deserves its unpublished fate, but that is quite valuable nonetheless because in it Anderson will explicitly carve out a rudimentary portrait of the grotesques.

. . .

Writing one of the few critical pieces ever published on *Talbot Whittingham*, Walter B. Rideout aptly summarized the feelings of generations of readers familiar with Sherwood Anderson's writings when he pondered the "aesthetic quantum jump" Anderson had made between his first two published novels and *Winesburg, Ohio*.[12] Rideout further addressed this "puzzling aspect" of Anderson's career by pointing out that Anderson was still revising these two novels while he was in the midst of writing his *Winesburg* tales. Rideout went on to argue that the unpublished *Talbot Whittingham*, much of which was penned just before Anderson started the *Winesburg* tales, shows a clearer "passage" to *Winesburg* than do the first novels. As the preceding discussion illustrates, there are reasons to disagree with Rideout's implicit dismissal of the first two novels. But Anderson's unpublished novel does show, in several ways, a close relationship to *Winesburg*. A seriously flawed work, it nevertheless is remarkable for documenting Anderson's progressively self-conscious exploration of the condition that he finally names in this work as the grotesque.

More important than the mere term itself, however, is the meaning with which Anderson invests the word "grotesque." In his early works he uses the term merely as a descriptive adjective; the condition to which the term would later apply remains unnamed until it appears with frenetic frequency in the latter half of *Talbot Whittingham*. Obviously Anderson developed the more symbolic use of the term while he was in Chicago, as several scholars have conjectured.[13] Perhaps the most important influence on him at this time was a free-verse play, *Grotesques: A Decoration in Black and White*, produced in Chicago in late 1915 only weeks before Anderson wrote "The Book of the Grotesque" and probably during the period in which he introduced the term *grotesque* in *Talbot Whittingham*. Although there is no extant evidence that Anderson knew this play, the timing of its appearance is uncanny, particularly since Anderson adopted the term grotesque in his own work soon after its production.

In an introduction to his annotated edition of *Talbot Whittingham*, Gerald Nemanic traces the sporadic history of the text's composition; some of his conclusions lend credence to the contention that Anderson underwent a transformation as he was composing *Talbot* that would not come to fruition until he turned his attention from novel writing and commenced what would become the *Winesburg* stories. Advancing on Harry Hansen's assertion that Anderson wrote *Talbot* in Ohio during the same period in which he wrote the first drafts of *Windy* and *Marching Men*,[14] Nemanic argues that the first parts of *Talbot*, where the action is set in New York and Ohio, were no doubt written before 1912; the last two sections, set in Chicago, he speculates to have been written between 1913 and 1916. He makes this estimate based on several incidents in the novel that parallel Anderson's experiences during his Chicago Renaissance years, for example, the Christ–Nietzsche debates in the novel and the content of the narrator's and Whittingham's musings on artistic theories.[15] Curiously missing from Nemanic's conjectures is any mention of the 1915 *Grotesques* or of the rather sudden appearance in *Talbot* of the self-named grotesques. Anderson was probably still working on *Talbot* into early 1916.[16]

The abrupt, lurching changes in the story's plot also suggest a later date of composition for the second half of the book. As Nemanic relates it, the early pages of the novel are missing but can be reconstructed from references throughout the book and from a reader's report by Marietta D. Finlay.[17] In brief: during his first twelve years Whittingham lives in New York amidst an "abnormal, sickly atmosphere," where his unsuccessful parents "aspired to holding a salon where young art might be duly appreciated."[18] Under somewhat bizarre circumstances, Whittingham moves to Mirage, a small Ohio town, in the care of Billy Bustard, a baker and cripple who had been his mother's patron. From this point on we have the extant manuscript, which goes on to relate (in the book's greatest detail) Whittingham's years in Mirage, where he spends most of his time loafing and brooding (and where he has his initial sexual experiences), while picking up valuable advice from Bruce Harvey, who races horses. His Mirage days come to an end when Billy's father, Tom Bustard, returns to town and plans to remove Whittingham from Billy's patronage. As told in affirming tones by the narrator (who professes to be a longtime friend of our protagonist), Whittingham murders Tom Bustard and leaves town unscathed on the pretense that the deed was done in self defense.

31

En route to Chicago, Whittingham meets an engaging woman from Indiana, a former schoolteacher who is an aspiring artist; she will reappear sporadically throughout Whittingham's Chicago's years and finally near the end of the novel be identified as Lucile Bearing. In Chicago Whittingham spends several years alternating between careers as a sparring partner at a boxing ring and an aspiring artist. Never does the narrator elaborate on what Whittingham actually writes. In book 4 Whittingham has a vision in the midst of his frequent perambulations around the city that formally introduces and names the downtrodden victims of modern life as grotesques. However, in a long digression from the plot, Whittingham becomes an advertising writer under the tutelage of a gifted ad man named Billows Turner. Eventually, though, after becoming a material success, Whittingham resumes his former contemplations on the grotesques, especially after witnessing an ongoing dispute between coworkers on the merits of Christ and Nietzsche. Inspired by Christ's teaching, "Let the dead bury the dead," Whittingham launches into a scheme whereby he and Turner sell cemetery plots to a target audience composed of all the grotesques in society. Whittingham gains material profits from the sales plus a newfound appreciation of society's defeated members.

In the last book of the novel, Whittingham encounters Adelaide Brown, who at first appears to be another "strong woman" like Sue Rainey and Margaret Ormsby from Anderson's first two novels. However, Whittingham exposes her as an artistic poseur, at which time Lucile Bearing, with an escort, coincidentally makes her final appearance. Defeated in her quest to be an artist, it is Lucile who is the true strong woman, someone who is strengthened from her defeat by life. Then, in one of the most contrived scenes Anderson ever created, Lucile and Whittingham walk outside into the rainy night while Whittingham recounts a dream he recently had about her in which she stands before him in front of a fireplace, soaked by rain, her clothes glistening from the background fire. Lucile's escort interrupts this reverie, shoots her, and runs away. Whittingham and Lucile return to her apartment, he all the while ruminating about himself while Lucile is slowly dying from her gunshot wound. When they finally reach her apartment, Whittingham enters first, leaving Lucile outside, so that he can rearrange the flat to resemble the setting of his dream. Enter Lucile, who, standing before the fireplace, glistens from the firelight, and then collapses in death. Finding beauty in such a death, Whittingham feels as "though in a dream he saw the purpose of his life in a new aspect. A keen, almost overpowering sense of the hidden beauty came over him. And he knew that the quest of beauty was to be for him the end in life."[19] The story thus ends with Whittingham poised to become yet another truth seeker, as were Anderson's previous novelistic heroes.

It is genuinely difficult to try to describe what is going on in the novel through a brief summary with the frequent shifts in the storyline and the emphases on so many newly introduced aspects of Whittingham's life and career. There is a lack of coherence or sense of direction throughout most of the work. Whereas in his childhood Sam McPherson strives to perfect his business skills in order to leave town and Beaut McGregor simply desires to flee his town because of his hatred of his fellow townsfolk, Whittingham's early years in Mirage are marked by no such goals. While freeloading off his benefactor, he merely feels superior to his peers but without having any sense of purpose. His murder of Tom Bustard is a transparent means of his demonstrating such superiority and providing a quick opportunity to leave town. Even Whittingham's early years in Chicago are marked by his transitory lifestyle: he passes the time boxing and simultaneously feeding his (and apparently his creator's) fascination with being a Nietzschean Superman.

If the plot up until this point meanders, there is nonetheless thematic continuity carried over from Anderson's first two novels, a thematic continuity that prefigures the introduction of the grotesques. Late in the second book, for instance, after Whittingham murders Tom Bustard, the intrusive narrator endorses his actions, explaining, "I am telling you the story of the growth and development of a master artist and one does not become the master artist who hesitates to throw the dice of life" (132). He goes on to say that many individuals are born who "have the vision of perfection and beauty that is in the eye of the artist, but produce no beauty. Hesitating, these figures stand as upon the very threshold of existence. Having quite clearly in the mind the vision or the act that is beautiful, they do not act but look into the distance, lost in dreams" (132). As in his first two novels, Anderson again is toying with the notion of true artists being great men who transcend the ruck of humanity, those who hesitate and "look into the distance, lost in dreams." His attention is still riveted on great figures—this time explicitly on the artist—while he dismisses the feeble masses.

As in his first two novels, Anderson here continues in this vein as Whittingham settles in Chicago and finds the urban dwellers there to be no different from the townsfolk in Mirage: "The men Talbot saw about him seemed pigmies when he thought of his own wit and cheekiness. . . . The boy was disappointed to find them not the giants he had half expected" (146). Like Anderson's other protagonists, Whittingham develops the habit of wandering the Chicago streets looking at people, behavior that draws the narrator's approval: "How fortunate for our Talbot that he stood looking instead of burying himself in the mass and getting fixed upon his face that eager, meaningless look" (158). In spite of his eventual epiphany concerning his mission to give voice to the grotesques, Whittingham remains an aloof figure through the book's conclusion, persisting there in talking about himself to Lucile Bearing even while she is fatally wounded.

But just as Beaut McGregor was suddenly struck with the plight of the defeated masses while walking the streets, so too does Whittingham experience such a moment; the difference, however, is in how closely worded the latter's experience is to many of the grotesques' experiences in *Winesburg*. It is notable, however, that unlike the case with Sam McPherson's and McGregor's radical transformations, nothing in *Talbot Whittingham* prepares us for Whittingham's.

One night, in the midst of one of his perambulations, Whittingham is struck by the power of a "new sensation": "All the men and women he had ever known seemed to press in about him, with their eyes and their hands they plead with him. 'Be the voice for us,' they seemed to say. . . . 'Help us that we may make ourselves understood, that all men and all women may make themselves understood'" (162). The plea of these individuals (who are still not identified as grotesques) clearly prefigures the plaintive need of the *Winesburg* grotesques to communicate their troubles and somehow transcend grotesqueness. In this work, however, Anderson fumbles after Whittingham's revelation. Although now we are told that Whittingham finally sees the downtrodden whom he passes in his walks—"not only the bodies but the living souls of men and women walking in the streets" (163)—Anderson still seems unprepared to focus attention on these defeated people. Instead, he returns to his preoccupation with artistic great men, as the ensuing scene in which Whittingham meets up with Lucile Bearing illustrates. Lucile, who by now is a defeated artist, reaffirms his newfound revelation that the great artist must give voice to the masses: "He must make the world understand in him what there is in all men and women and what, in their own persons, they cannot understand" (176). From here the plot lurches in other directions, taking Whittingham into the advertising business. It is not until later in book 4, the section written in Chicago probably just before he began the *Winesburg* tales, that Anderson himself seems to experience an epiphanic moment of insight concerning the grotesques.

Leading up to this moment is a protracted scene involving the debates discussed earlier between two of Whittingham's coworkers over the merits of Nietzsche and Christ. The "disciple of Nietzsche" dismisses Christ's teachings as mere sentimentality while touting a new creed of stark individualism: "Wives, families, churches, beliefs, all old associations should be brushed aside. There must come now a period of intense individualism" (211). The advocate of Christ admonishes the Nietzschean for relying too much on "his brain, his foolish brain filled with rules and axioms and laws. His brain tells him to look with contempt upon Christ's ideas of infinite pity" (209). Adapting a line from scripture, the "disciple of Christ" declares, "The world is a dead place filled with the unburied dead" (211), a line that has a striking effect on Whittingham. Left finally alone, musing on a bridge during a steady drizzle, he listens to the falling drops and utters, "It is the footsteps of the little God of the grotesque that I hear. . . . They are everywhere, down in the city they sit all day at desks along the wall. When their bodies are all drawn out of shape, when they have grown old and fat and unlovely they are turned loose to rule the world" (215). Thus Anderson uses the term "grotesque" for the first time as a collective noun, and from this point until the end of the novel he will use the term repeatedly, seemingly grappling with the concept as he goes along.

The way Anderson explores this newly coined concept for the rest of the novel is laborious and quite literal, but it is important to understand its basic components. In *Talbot Whittingham*, grotesques are those who lead defeated lives, people who are exhausted and weary with living to the extent that for them there is no beauty in the world. Nevertheless they trudge on with their lives, struggling against everyday obstacles, hoping (but barely) to strike back against those forces that keep them down or at least articulate such feelings in either words or deeds thereby attaining some kind of peace and understanding about themselves. As Rideout describes it,

Grotesqueness, in sum, is a universal but outward condition of the world which both defeats men's dreams and separates them as individuals; beauty is a universal but inward condition which exists beyond defeat, binds individuals into a community, and when liberated by the artist's insight, emerges out of defeat in the form of art.[20]

Anderson has Whittingham experiment with his newfound realization of the grotesques immediately after his moment of insight, and both protagonist and author seem preoccupied with a literal application of the term. We are told that six people who overheard the Nietzschean's speeches and who were moved by them approach Whittingham that night. Of the six, only one person's encounter with Whittingham is described. A waitress, who is continually harassed by her patrons, tells him that she suddenly feels the urge to actually beat every man in the restaurant where she works: "She would make a wreck of the place. After that she would run into the street and begin anew. Her figure should come to stand for something. Everywhere she would beat down men. She would make her protests felt and understood" (219). Whittingham runs his hand over her face and body and informs her that she is alive: "I feel the life in you. You are a grotesque living thing" (220); but he also adds that she is not "beautifully alive" (222). Whittingham's initial response to his epiphany is indeed backward looking: he proposes to "get through the grotesque" by murdering someone, a perfect stranger. As he sees it, "If life was a grotesque thing, a thing that twisted and maimed men, filling the world with babblers, then, he thought, he would do away with at least one walking, talking, pretending, grotesque manifestation of life" (223). These are hardly the thoughts of an empathetic artist.

After deciding against murdering a drunken merchant, Whittingham then hatches his cemetery scheme, quite literally applying the disciple of Christ's belief that "the world is a dead place filled with the unburied dead" (211–12), by buying up plots and selling them to the living for their eventual burials. Besides making a tidy profit from this venture, Whittingham suddenly decides (for the first time in the book without the narrator's intrusions) that he will become a writer. At this moment, while feeling that "all in the world were dead and that in the future he would make it a rule of his life to be as hard as adamant toward the dead" (236), he is struck by an intimate scene of two lovers outside his bedroom window; his Nietzschean thoughts of being superior to the grotesques are dashed suddenly because of this observation. He intimates that in the midst of the harshness of life, one might yet find beauty and understanding. He will apply this new insight (again quite exactly) when he encounters Lucile Bearing for the last time.

In this scene, Whittingham has been lecturing to the artistic poseur Adelaide Brown in a restaurant, sharing his fresh insights that people do not see beauty in the world and saying to her, "[The] world is the abode of the grotesque. I am a grotesque and you are one" (248). Continuing his one-way conversation, he asks her, "Why do I not strive for beauty? . . . Why do we insist upon being grotesques?" (253). As if in response to his question, Lucile enters, appearing beaten down by life, and Whittingham recognizes that she embodies the solution: "Here was the death in life that was not death, that was conscious, defiant, grinning" (257). He tells Adelaide that "we must get past the grotesque" and that the "grotesque is like a wall" (258), whereupon he dismisses her and turns to Lucile, who, he feels, has transcended grotesqueness. When they enact his dream setting at her apartment, the narrator explains its significance for us: "The Indiana school teacher who had come into the city only to be defeated had conquered defeat" (272). Now won over to the "infinite pity" of Christ instead of the hard shallowness of Nietzsche, Whittingham is thus prepared to be the master artist, an Emersonian poet of sorts, for the grotesques.

Judging from the novel's preoccupation with the concept of grotesques in the latter half of the story, it seems evident that Anderson himself must have been inspired by something while he was working on the book and that he began unsuccessfully exploring this concept as he brought the novel to its hasty conclusion. He shows a fixation with the notion that the grotesques are like the living dead, virtually powerless to strike through the "wall" to "get past the grotesque." Language, too, deters rather than aids in communicating their condition, as when the narrator explains that the grotesque fill the "world with babblers" (223). And, of course, it is implicit that a nexus of power sources in society creates the milieu for the grotesques. Each of these ideas will evolve intelligibly when Anderson takes up the *Winesburg* tales. In *Talbot Whittingham*, however, they are clumsily and obviously rendered in both the development of Whittingham's character and the intrusive narration of the story.

As to what the "something" was that inspired Anderson to consider the concept of the grotesque, it may be worthwhile to explore at some length the play referred to earlier for clues as to why Anderson finally turned his attention to the subject of the downtrodden rather than to Nietzschean great men.

Grotesques, by Cloyd Head, premiered at the Chicago Little Theatre on November 16, 1915.[21] It is an experimental play in which its main character, Capulchard, creates several vignettes involving grotesques—figures who are literally lifeless until he calls on them to perform for the audience. Capulchard addresses the audience throughout, regarding them as gods for whose entertainment he presents these vignettes. As Marilyn Atlas points out, "[Capulchard's] major relationship is not with [the grotesques] but with the audience whose approval and complicity he desires."[22] The action takes place in front of a framed, monochromatic background consisting of minimalist renderings of

37

natural objects (a stream, the moon, an owl, for instance), and on each side of the framed background is a dark gauze; behind this gauze the grotesques lie inanimate.

Throughout the vignettes of this short play, Capulchard demonstrates his powers of manipulation over the grotesques: creating scenes (or *designs,* as he calls them), giving the grotesques roles to play and suggesting lines for them to speak, changing scenes when the grotesques do not perform to his liking. All of this, he maintains, is for the "amusement" of the audience (3), although it is clear that he certainly takes pleasure in controlling the grotesques, who for most of the play remain unable to control their own actions. As he tells the audience at one point, "It's naught to these Grotesques, unconscious strings / Scraped into melody, but else inert" (5). When a design seems to falter, Capulchard simply extricates the grotesque with a nod or movement of his arm, whereby the figure collapses like a marionette behind the screen. Indeed, the grotesques are intended to perform like puppets with "unconscious strings," speaking Capulchard's suggested lines in abstract, flat tones, and progressing across the stage in "conventionalized movements." In each design their assigned roles change instantaneously upon Capulchard's directions; even their original "characters" are vague abstractions, such as Man-motive, Woman-motive, and Girl-motive.

It is when Capulchard enters into a design as a player that the grotesques become sentient beings. Anticipating that the audience wants more "tang," Capulchard as "vicar" over the grotesques appears in a design as an "ex-officio spectre" (12). The Man-motive becomes conscious that Capulchard is addressing someone off stage—the audience—whom the Man-motive supposes to be gods. Told that his very presence is to appease the audience, the Man-motive pays them homage: "I will give thanks unto our gods and plead / Of them protection: I am their Grotesque" (14), whereupon he erects a crude altar. The Man-motive, having by now a semblance of consciousness, nevertheless makes himself complicit in his subjection, declaring, "The gods watch over us, they guard us well; / They have no other thought but for our good" (20). After an exchange of roles between the Girl-motive and the Woman-motive, an exchange that causes him frustration, the Man-motive appeals to the audience to intercede. Capulchard, sensing a threat to his own power, reminds the Man-motive, "The gods are kind, but wish to be amused. / Obey the decoration: be not like / The marionette who learned that there were strings / And, seeking independence, severed them" (22).

Undaunted, the Man-motive tells the Woman-motive that "We'll make our own design" (23). But Capulchard quickly alters the design and, to reassure the audience, tells them,

> Grotesques are something that must be surpassed.
> But you, their gods, for whom they are create [*sic*]—
> Ultimate critics in Olympian chairs—
> Shall laugh at their weak struggle to be—gods? (24)

His control is threatened again, though, for the Man-motive and Woman-motive renew their intent to weave their own design, heedless of Capulchard or the audience. With what control he still possesses, however, Capulchard instills in them fear of completely breaking free: the Woman-motive tells her partner, "Beyond is naught, / Except the gods," to which the Man-motive, now terrified, responds, "Do you not feel their eyes— / Eyes that stare, waiting?" (27) He adds, "Those ancient, staring eyes that will outlive / The moon and stars compel us to submit" (28). Realizing their defeat, the Woman-motive admits that "Whatever we do / Ends as he [Capulchard] planned."

Their defeat becomes a Pyrrhic victory for Capulchard, however, for they consciously submit but with a willful defiance. The Man-motive announces to the audience, "I / Am a Grotesque; we will no longer bow, / The prey of gods!" whereupon he destroys the altar he had earlier built (29). Receiving no punishment from this act, he further declares to the audience, "Hear, / O ye gods who brought us into life, / We fling defiance: give us freedom!" Capulchard's only recourse is to literally commence dismantling the set and thus bring an end to the design and the play, leaving the grotesques "Caught in the void: we'll sweep the canvas clear. . . . / For naught is permanent—excepting change" (30).

As already indicated, no evidence exists showing that Anderson attended the play, read its reviews, or even noticed it when it was published in *Poetry* nearly a year later. But the thematic similarities of Head's grotesques and the grotesques that Anderson had begun developing in *Talbot Whittingham*, and soon in the *Winesburg* tales, are astonishing. In *Grotesques* we are presented with characters who are lifeless until they are assigned roles to play and lines to speak. Unconscious role players, they assume their parts at the whim of both an individual (Capulchard) and an anonymous power source (the complicit audience), and their performance is closely monitored by both. Achieving consciousness, they permit themselves to continue being subjected until,

39

reaching a point of abject frustration, they attempt to break through their confined condition; but, fearing the unknown consequences of such an act, they willingly submit to their role, which is now made more intolerable because they are conscious of their subjection. Removed from the context of the play, this paradigm could apply nearly verbatim to the context of the *Winesburg* grotesques.

To hypothesize that Anderson had indeed a close familiarity with this play is irresistible; after all, his literary circle in Chicago had strong ties with the people involved with the Little Theatre. As Atlas argues, it was commonplace for those involved with the theater, such as its producer, Maurice Browne, as well as other artists and intellectuals, to meet regularly to discuss "new ideas and manuscripts."[23] Perhaps Anderson was already acquainted with the play before it premiered. His near obsessive fascination with the concept of the grotesque midway in a novel whose plot had been meandering up until that point echoes Head's treatment of defeated characters that the playwright called grotesques. Grappling with this new concept, to which he had heretofore given only glancing consideration, Anderson has his protagonist explore different directions: he has him ponder murdering a grotesque; then he has him sell burial plots to the grotesques; finally he has him realize that the grotesques can transcend their condition and find beauty by means of persevering in their defeat and that he, as a master artist, can articulate this experience.

To continue with this hypothesis, perhaps Head's attention specifically to the manipulation of the voiceless grotesques contributed to Anderson's own reconsideration of his subject matter. Perhaps Anderson realized that his repeated attempts to write about heroic protagonists had devolved into pat, formulaic story lines, that his passing attention to society's downtrodden merited reconsideration, and that by focusing on the inarticulate masses in society he could begin experimenting with a more evocative style of narration. But before this hypothesis spirals too far into the realm of speculation, Head's *Grotesques* is not the prima facie sole missing link between Anderson's flawed first novels and his masterpiece *Winesburg, Ohio;* however, this play may have provided a creative spark for Anderson, leading to ideas that he began clumsily working out in *Talbot Whittingham* and then executed with precision in *Winesburg.* This hypothesis furnishes several intelligible pieces to the puzzle of how Anderson came to *Winesburg.*

In his first novels, Anderson began to explore the conditions and characteristics of the modern grotesque and to experiment with the elusive vagaries of language. This chapter has attempted to extend Gadamer's "fusion of horizons" for our understanding of *Winesburg* so that we might better appreciate how Anderson forged a modernist classic that prefigured our postmodernist age. As Rideout has shown, Anderson did not make an immediate transition from *Talbot Whittingham* to *Winesburg, Ohio*. While still working on the latter, he toyed with different stories about Talbot Whittingham, each ending up as discarded sheets.[24] But in December 1915 he had turned over some previously discarded Talbot sheets and began to write "The Book of the Grotesque" and thus graduated from his apprenticeship as a writer.

CHAPTER THREE

Getting the "Thing Needed"

THE MODERN GROTESQUE
IN *WINESBURG, OHIO*

We could say that every period has its own postmodernism.[1]

It should be clear from the previous chapter that when he came to write the tales that would fill *Winesburg, Ohio*, Sherwood Anderson did not suddenly hit upon the idea of fusing an interest in the modern grotesque with an understanding of the inefficacy of language. He had already begun depicting the milieu of the modern grotesque in his early novels and showed a growing awareness of the indeterminacy of meaning in language. With *Winesburg*, however, he successfully explored the close relationship of these two issues not only in the content of the tales but also in the telling of the tales.

It is important to note too that with *Winesburg* Anderson immersed himself in the short-story form rather than in another novel. This newfound attention is no doubt partly due to the practical demands of his having a full-time job writing advertising copy; but it also signals Anderson's awareness of the stunted, fragmentary nature of modern American life. What ultimately makes his early novels failures is his stolid adherence to a conventional plotting and telling of his stories. With the *Winesburg* tales (as in many of his better short stories after *Winesburg*) he replaces both artificial plotting and objective narration with incomplete and subjective glimpses into people's lives. It is really a moot point to enter into the decades' long debate of whether the book is a novel or not. What is more important is to realize that with *Winesburg* we have a series of tales related primarily by the collective entity of the town and its surrounding environs. One can read the book thematically as a depiction of George Willard's rite of passage into adulthood, but to do so would

43

44

belie the fact that it does not offer us a linear narrative of George's development into adulthood and would necessitate overlooking many stories in which
George plays little or no part. Yet the book is not a collection of unrelated
stories either, like *Death in the Woods and Other Stories*. There is, then, in
terms of a coherent narrative only a relative relationship between each of the
stories in *Winesburg*. This I call a harmonious paradox because, just as "The
Book of the Grotesque" provides at best a tenuous schematic for the whole
book, the book itself is tenuously integrated. In addition, its fragmented organization mirrors the very content of the book—subjective portraits of numerous stunted, inchoate individuals. What makes *Winesburg* stand apart
dramatically from Anderson's earlier fiction is neither its provocative content
nor its insights into language but its sustained integration of the two in a
form that fully complements that integration.

As early as *Windy McPherson's Son*, Anderson began etching a modern social context, in both town and city, in which people lead lives under subjection to various power sources, either succumbing to social pressures or subjecting themselves. In *Marching Men* he began exploring the inefficacy of
language, particularly how it could be manipulated to mold personal identity.
In *Talbot Whittingham* he seemed almost to stumble on a conscious recogni-
tion of subjected and defeated humanity, whom he called grotesques. But in
Winesburg, Ohio, he skillfully integrates the various strands introduced in his
earlier works into a powerful portrait of modern America. He works in a suitable form, the short story; he sketches a deceptively simple paradigm of the
modern grotesque in his introductory tale—nearly a formula through which
he consciously undermines any absolute truthfulness; and he offers subjective
portraits of the various manifestations of grotesqueness. Like Melville's "Doubloon" chapter in *Moby-Dick*, "The Book of the Grotesque" establishes parameters for interpretation and meaning while undercutting its own textual
authority to provide conclusive answers to the questions it raises. Working
within fragmentary tales, employing a style of narration that constantly questions the veracity of what is narrated, and focusing on characters who are
incapable of effective articulation in their quest for meaning, Anderson creates in *Winesburg* an exemplary precursor to postmodernism.

Critics have studied the frustration and inarticulateness of the characters
since the book's publication in 1919. But in spite of the rise of structuralist and
poststructuralist theory over the last thirty or so years, the book has not been
adequately approached from a postmodernist perspective.[2] As Monica Flu-

dernik has observed, Anderson has not been traditionally regarded as "'difficult' enough; indeed, the ostensible simplicity of his prose has become almost proverbial. As a consequence, Anderson's writing has not seemed to invite the aid of literary theory, which critics in considering other modernist texts have generally found indispensable." In accordance with Walter Rideout's comment that *Winesburg*'s "simplicity . . . [is] of a complicated kind," the book will here be examined using the methodology discussed in chapter 1.[3] Specifically, this will entail a two-pronged approach that tests some of Foucault's theories of power forces and the submission of the individual while also examining how Anderson undermines the veracity of his storytelling by drawing our attention over and over again to the instability of language. We shall therefore approach *Winesburg* as a series of unconventional case studies of the modern grotesque that present diverse scenarios under which individuals fall prey to normalized codes of behavior; in addition, we shall study the text as a primer on how not to trust language as a means of capturing or conveying objective truths.

Although the narrator of "The Book of the Grotesque" self-consciously backs away from giving us a concrete definition of the grotesque, we can glean from his tentative rendering of the old man's "elaborate theory" something akin to a diagnosis of a disease. People snatch up truths—abstract concepts related to living in a social context—and become grotesques by trying to mold their lives rigidly by them. As discussed in chapter 1, these truths all entail individuals' practicing them in human society, presumably in order to live contented, fulfilling lives. Irving Howe mistakenly criticizes the tale for suggesting that "the grotesques are victims of their own wilful fanaticism."[4] As this tale and the others following it suggest, the grotesques are sometimes responsible for their own submission, but in other instances they seem to cave in to pressures exerted by outside forces. They may indeed seek out the truths of their own accord, but they are also *expected to do so* by various sources in society. In essence, the truths are imitable formulas for living the good life *in society*. But these characters do not achieve the good life; in fact, they usually become failures by society's standards. Often, in recognizing their disappointments, such people also feel a betrayal of sorts, in particular a betrayal by language's failure to provide a sustained meaning for them. Language gives the truths the air of actuality, and when embracing truths reduces them to grotesques, these individuals implicitly reject language as a means of providing meaning. However, the plight that such characters experience involves their attempts to find empathy and understanding from others, seemingly as

45

a way of transcending the grotesque; as the ensuing tales show, these attempts most often involve the characters trying to communicate via language. Hence, most of the characters focused on in *Winesburg* remain frustrated after such attempts. In depicting his characters' failed experiences, Anderson suggests throughout the book a diagnosis of grotesqueness. Unlike his previous novels, though, *Winesburg* does not provide a definitive cure; in fact, consistent with the book's wariness of the reliability of language, Anderson provides at best only an intuitive cure near the end of the book.

We can begin an examination of the stories by considering the kinds of truths exposed and their relationship to the community. As the old writer in "The Book of the Grotesque" contrasts one abstract truth with another (for instance, virginity and passion, wealth and poverty), so too might we study the tales themselves. The following discussion orders the tales according to several key influences on the characters: the overt presence of the town; general popular myths concerning success or adulthood that originate from outside the town; religion; societal expectations concerning sexuality or marriage; and finally the ways in which these various influences affect George Willard. These influences all emerge from various segments in society, and no single truth, or imitable formula, pervades the tales. Rather, they form an amalgam of ideological constructs that the protagonists of the tales either succumb to or willfully embrace.

.   .   .

The influence of the town itself is manifested throughout *Winesburg*. The town often serves as critical eyes that evaluate and pass judgment on individuals. Whether singularly (as in Banker White's wife) or collectively, the town functions like the operation of Foucault's Panopticon, by holding up individuals in relief to scrutinize their behavior, as the individuals themselves submit to the test of the town's normalized standards. As Anderson shows, whether these standards are clearly identified or merely assumed, they are nonetheless evacuated of their intended meaning, serving instead as a leveling form of discipline. In this context, the "truth" shall not set one free.

In "Hands," for instance, Wing Biddlebaum is literally and figuratively isolated from the town, and he is fully conscious that his isolation is equated to punishment for his past transgressions. Living in a crumbling house that "stood *near* the edge of a ravine *near* the town of Winesburg, Ohio," (emphasis mine) that is also separated from the "public highway" by a "long field,"[5] Wing is totally ostracized from society. As the narrator relates, "Wing Biddlebaum, forever frightened and beset by a ghostly band of doubts, did not think of himself as in any way a part of the life of the town where he had lived for twenty years" (11). Nonverbal communication with his hands had been Wing's means of expression when he was a teacher decades earlier, and ironically his hands had become his "distinguishing feature" in Winesburg—but as a commodity rather than as an instrument of intuitive understanding. Formerly a sensitive and nurturing teacher, Wing is recast in Winesburg into an inconsequential trophy object: "Winesburg was proud of the hands of Wing Biddlebaum in the same spirit in which it was proud of Banker White's new stone house and Wesley Moyer's bay stallion, Tony Tip" (13). Reduced to a commodified curio, Wing is also psychologically alienated from society.

The narrator intensifies Wing's present alienation in Winesburg by contrasting it to his former life as a teacher, when his hands were used as instruments of creativity and inspiration. In the Pennsylvania school, "under the caress of his hands doubt and disbelief went out of the minds of the boys and they began . . . to dream" (15). Dreams in this tale and throughout *Winesburg* are regarded positively by the narrator; but dreams, like the concept of understanding, cannot be captured precisely in language. Because of their elusiveness, dreams can lend themselves to misinterpretation, as happens in the story when the "half-witted boy" related his sexual "dreams as facts" (15). Anderson suggests, however, that Adolph Myers's penchant for using his hands as a means of expression had already been suspect by the town, when the narrator comments, "Hidden, shadowy doubts that had been in men's minds concerning Adolph Myers were galvanized into beliefs" (15). Like Winesburg (or, by extension, like any societal organization), the Pennsylvania town is suspicious of such communication because it cannot be neatly gauged and assessed, and accordingly, people like Adolph who resort to such expression also raise suspicions. Deemed a pervert,[6] Adolph Myers is run out of town not knowing exactly why, except that "the hands must be to blame" (16). The town thus instills in him a similar distrust of his hands.

In Winesburg, Wing lives a frustrated and baffled life: the "hands alarmed their owner" (12) because of his past negative experience, and yet, recast into a commodity, they are now prized by the town. His primary means of expression inhibited, yet feeling nonetheless the need to communicate with George Willard, Wing is reduced to "striving to put into words the ideas that had been accumulated by his mind during long years of silence" (12). It is not surprising that in his talks with George, Wing emphasizes to the young man the need to dream and to "shut your ears to the roaring of the voices" (14). Wing recognizes that his life is stifled and frustrated, and he desires to express this, both to teach George and no doubt to achieve some kind of understanding. However, just when Wing abandons his attempts to express himself in language and begins to "caress the boy," his instilled fear of his hands intrudes; he succumbs to the lockstep mentality of the Pennsylvania town and quickly dismisses the boy. The life-creating force that was "diffused, not centralized" in Wing (15) remains subsumed under the superficial role that the town of Winesburg has since assigned to him. Having submitted to the judgment of the Pennsylvania town, Wing lives his life in Winesburg as if he is still under surveillance.

Interestingly, just as Wing's preferred means of effecting understanding is nonverbal, the narration, too, seems to imply that genuine understanding comes not from definitive verbal articulation but from a more intuitive means. Here and throughout the book, the narration reminds the reader of its unreliability as a means of relating objective reality. At times the narrator even seems to display a concern about being watched and judged similar to what Wing experiences. For instance, as the narrator explains that men like Wing who have such affection for their students are "not unlike the finer sort of women in their love of men," he then immediately qualifies his statement, saying, "And yet that is but crudely stated. It needs the poet there" (15). The narration draws attention to itself as being an insufficient means of describing Wing's love for his students and of conveying the "truth" of Wing Biddlebaum. Here form and content complement each other.

In contrast to Wing Biddlebaum's plight, in "The Philosopher" we are presented with a character who consciously projects the appearance of being subjected to the town's surveillance and control while in actuality subjecting himself. Similar in this respect to Elmer Cowley in "'Queer,'" Dr. Parcival distinguishes himself, however, from Elmer by having experienced a childhood in which his identity was sharply influenced by the mind-set of the town, as personified particularly by both his mother and brother. With Parcival we can trace how a person amplifies an early pattern of behavior into a reactionary yet fixed philosophy of life.

As a resident of Winesburg, Parcival perceives himself as an aloof and superior figure. He tells Biff Carter in his lunchroom, "I am a man of distinction, you see" (33). During his many talks with George Willard, he frequently tries to impress the boy that he is a man of wealth and mystery. In effect, though, he manipulates language to project an image of himself that seems at odds with actual experience. He teases George's curiosity about his medical practice, for instance, when he explains why he has few patients. It is not because he lacks medical skill, he tells the boy: "The reason, you see, does not appear on the surface. It lies in fact in my character, which has, if you think about it, many strange turns" (32). He is evasive with George about his past experience as a reporter, telling him, "Perhaps I am trying to conceal my identity and don't want to be very definite. Have you ever thought it strange that I have money for my needs although I do nothing?" (33). He taunts George: "If you were a really smart newspaper reporter you would look me up." The purpose of his talks, he tells George, is "to fill [him] with hatred and contempt so that [he] will be a superior being" (36), much like himself.

This vaunted image of himself is in no way reflected in or affirmed by the town, however. Parcival, like Wash Williams in "Respectability" and Jesse Bentley in "Godliness," is as much a physical grotesque as he is a psychological one. His left eye twitches, his mouth is droopy, and he "always wore a dirty white waistcoat" (31). The narrator informs us that he was thrown in jail on his arrival in Winesburg for starting a drunken fight with a train employee. He becomes a figure largely ignored by the town. This is clearly shown in the conclusion of the tale, when Parcival refuses to attend to a fatally wounded child and anticipates that the town will descend on him in a posse and hang him. Parcival says to convince George, "What I have done will arouse the people of this town" (37). But, as the narrator states, "The useless cruelty of his refusal had passed unnoticed." Parcival is forced to confront this reality when his fear of being lynched is replaced by doubt, but he ends up wrapping himself even more closely within his self-spun illusion. His philosophy—"that everyone in the world is Christ and they are all crucified"—ends up ringing hollow, in light of the circumstances. Parcival's renewed fear of an eventual lynching is equally groundless.

In the end Parcival exposes himself to be a conflicted personality: he disregards the importance of material, sensual things (his physical appearance, the quality of the food he eats) while claiming for himself intrinsic worth (being a "man of distinction"). Yet for him that intrinsic worth can only be validated by the external sanction of the town. Parcival reveals the source of his frustrated identity when he relates his earlier life experiences to George. It is in this talk that he divulges his contempt for material things, particularly as they relate to the relationship between his mother and brother. As he describes it, his brother was a contemptible person who would taunt his family by leaving his pay on the kitchen table and then threaten them if they touched any of it. His clothes saturated with orange paint from his job as a railroad painter, the brother would remove the money over a period of days, seemingly spending it all on carousing and drinking. From the young Parcival's perspective, that of a minister-in-training, his brother was a thorough sensualist. And yet, he tells George, his mother loved his brother more than him, perhaps in large part because, in spite of his behavior, the brother provided the family with groceries and other material necessities. Detecting a disconnect between his brother's actions and the love his mother had for him, Parcival senses a similar disparity between his solemn role ministering at his father's death and the attention he receives at the asylum because of his temporary job of reporter. He tells George, "They treated me as though I was a king" (35) because the asylum administrators feared a scandal in the press. Parcival ultimately tries to convince himself of his innate worth because early in life he recognizes the shallowness of external social roles. His mother loves the unruly brother because he provides things for the house; the asylum administrators treat him with respect not because he is an aspiring minister but because they fear his lowly but potentially powerful position as a reporter.

Parcival also hints that he recognizes the shallowness of language, as when he relates to George how his brother would have laughed had he heard his solemn prayer over his dead father. With social titles devoid of meaning for him, so too are linguistic rituals, especially when they are garbled, as when Parcival prays over his father: "Let peace brood over this carcass" (35). His personality significantly shaped by such events, Parcival as an adult becomes a willful subject of the town; ironically, at the same time that he presents himself as a great man, he yet craves and needs the interest and validation of the town to confirm this image. He only resorts to his encomium to George ("everyone in the world is Christ and they are all crucified") after he realizes that the town has bestowed him with no such status. His philosophy ends up sounding as meaningless as his prayer over his father. In like fashion, the "adventure" that the narrator attributes to Parcival's actions with the dead child also seems to ring hollow. The "adventures" of other characters in the book typically involve a fleeting moment of insight for them; this is not the case with Parcival, who instead reaffirms his deluded image of himself. And George's naïveté, in believing that the doctor's tales "contained the very essence of truth" (33), only contributes to the irony.

Similar to Parcival is Joe Welling from "A Man of Ideas," who displays a hyperactive obsession with trying to ingratiate himself as a figure of attention in the town. Joe is a son of a "man of some dignity in the community, a lawyer and a member of state legislature" (77). His father was an important man of influence in the town, and Joe, too, wields some influence as the town's Standard Oil agent, a position secured for him by his father. Bestowed with a prominent position in the community, Joe nevertheless is compelled to make himself the center of attention wherever he goes. The town's reaction to him ranges from "amusement tempered by alarm" to "helpless annoyance" (78).

Joe repeatedly imposes himself on the town as a "man of ideas" by means of his unremitting use of words: "He was beset by ideas and in the throes of one of his ideas was uncontrollable. Words rolled and tumbled from his mouth" (77). The town regards him with either bemusement or weariness, yet in effect it has reduced Joe to being another town curio, like Wing Biddlebaum. Perhaps because he is relegated to the function of town "character," and because he feels the need to assert his own importance independent of his father's reputation, Joe disrupts every conversation he enters to draw attention to himself. In a drugstore where men are discussing horses, for instance, Joe diverts attention as soon as he enters, by "brushing the screen door violently aside." Not partaking in the conversation, he delivers a lengthy monologue about the water level of Wine Creek and then exits (78). He declares to George Willard that he should have the young man's job of reporter because he would be better at it, adding, though, that he makes more money as the town's oil agent. He then orders the reporter to take down a fresh idea of his, that the world is on fire. Not satisfied that this idea will catch on in the *Winesburg Eagle*, Joe concludes by saying that he should start his own newspaper: "I'd be a marvel. Everybody knows that" (80).

Everybody does not know that, however. In spite of his job and his self-conscious attempts to win the town's respect and admiration, Joe has a marginalized place in the community, like Doctor Parcival. His verbiage causes no admiration; instead, the town tolerates him at arm's length until he serves the superficial purpose of coaching the town baseball club. It is only in this role that "Joe began to win the respect of his townsmen" (80). In effect, the town takes the same kind of pride in Joe's success as a manager as it did in Wing Biddlebaum's prowess at berry-picking: his identity is commodified. Joe, however, sees his newfound role as baseball manager to be the perfect opportunity to indulge in his egocentric obsession, as when he coaches his players from first base:

"Now! Now! Now! Now!" shouted the excited man. "Watch me! Watch me! Watch me! Watch my fingers! Watch my hands! Watch my feet! Watch my eyes! Let's work together here! Watch me! In me you see all the movements of the game! Work with me! Work with me! Watch me! Watch me! Watch me!" (80)

With "his whole body quivering with excitement," it is Joe's hyperactive fixation with having others pay attention to him that makes him a successful manager, not his coaching skills, for the narrator tells us that such antics typically distracted and confused the opposing players.

But it is primarily because of this perfunctory role that Joe's affair with Sarah King sets the "town of Winesburg on edge." Overhearing his "protestations of love" to Sarah in presumably secluded locations (behind cemetery walls, from the shadows of trees at the fairgrounds) and spreading the gossip along Main Street, the town suddenly displays a probing and far-reaching level of surveillance when its interests are at stake. Disapproving of the King family, who were "not popular in Winesburg," the town titillates itself in "sensing a tragedy" about to ensue, although it does nothing to prevent such a calamity. In one of the few lighthearted moments in the book, though, the narrator describes how Joe apparently wins over the Kings, who are "absorbed, fascinated" with Joe's ideas (84).

Joe's marginalized position in the community is thus reinforced by his ability to hold court only with rank outsiders of the town. His obsessive drive to be the center of attention as a man of ideas succeeds only when that attention is severely narrow. Language fails to effect any meaningful understanding; Joe's stream of words neither challenges nor interests the town to any extent, and his self-absorption intensifies his ostracized position in the community. Like Dr. Parcival, Joe's behavior resembles Foucault's renderings of inmates or the insane who subject themselves to gain the approval of those who have the power to judge them. They do not succeed, and the unabated language they employ is ineffectual.

Faced with a situation diametrically opposed to Joe's is Seth Richmond in "The Thinker." Unlike Joe Welling, Seth is a silent presence in Winesburg. Because of his silence and aloofness from others, the town deems him "the deep one" (103). Throughout the story Seth displays doubts about both the efficacy of language and the integrity of social roles in the community. In sharp contrast to Joe Welling, Seth is continually disappointed in both words and work; he seems to discern that family and work and community are but hollowed ideals. As a result, he is cut off from the town but cannot find a viable alternative, and so he remains in static isolation. But with "The Thinker" Anderson does more than explore another perspective on the grotesques: he creates a tour de force of an organic merging of content and form. The very narration of "The Thinker" complements the doubts about language and ideology that Seth exhibits.

Seth's distrust of language and his distrust of social roles are intertwined, and the narration itself reinforces this distrust. Early in the story the narrator is almost too insistent that Seth's father was "extraordinarily admired by his neighbors" and was, according to his wife, Virginia, someone "whom all had instinctively loved" (99–100). But such accolades are undercut by the stories that circulated after the father's death, when he was shot in a fight brought about by a newspaper scandal concerning a possible affair he had had. This news is coupled with that of the family's being left penniless as a result of the father's poor business investments. Seth's mother, who "expected from all people certain conventional reactions to life" (101), entreats Seth not to believe the gossip about his father. The narration here thus instills instability in the tale: how true are the narrator's comments that the father was "extraordinarily admired" by the town, when he undermines such a conclusion by including the sordid stories—circulated by the town—surrounding his death? The reader is therefore placed in Seth's shoes, for we share the same kind of doubt that he displays.

Virginia contributes to Seth's doubts by trying to instill in him a sense of pride in family and self that is frequently at odds with actual experience. The narrator, alternating the point of view from Virginia's to the town's to Seth's, perpetuates the feeling of uncertainty that pervades the tale. In characterizing the disjointed relationship between mother and son, the narrator tells us, "The truth was that the son thought with remarkable clearness and the mother did not" (101). Presumably this statement mirrors not only Virginia's attitude but also the town's attitude, because later the narrator describes the "respect with which men and boys instinctively greeted" Seth. But such sentiments, which seem to affirm Seth's social status as the "deep one," are immediately undercut by the narrator, who, in the same passage, tells us that Seth "was not what the men of the town, and even his mother, thought him to be. No great underlying purpose lay back of his habitual silence, and he had no definite plan for his life" (103). Seth is imbued with a social title that, like the townsfolk's and his family's assessments, is without meaning.

The reader is made privy to this insight, and Seth seems to realize it as well. From his many observations of the townsfolk, he repeatedly confirms his suspicions that they are either fakes or blustering distractions. In the beginning of the tale, he finds the young berry pickers to be a "chattering crowd" that "sometimes irritated him sharply" (99). He stands aside from his boyhood peers, whom he deems "noisy and quarrelsome" (103). He overhears a heated political debate between Tom Willard and some of his guests, and he labels the hotel keeper "windy old Tom Willard" (104). "Depressed by the thought that he was not a part of the life of his own town" (106), Seth seeks out George Willard to talk to, but he soon relegates George to the same low status as the other vapid townsfolk. George's behavior aptly provokes Seth to make such a conclusion.

Ensconced in his room at the Willard Hotel, George does not solicit conversation from Seth but instead rhapsodizes about what he thinks is the ideal writer's life. The narrator, assuming Seth's point of view, describes George's job as reporter to be a series of running around town, like "an excited dog," writing "little facts" on his pad for the newspaper. George's projection of himself to the town as a budding writer "had given him a place of distinction in Winesburg," as he tells Seth when he visits him. The narration here affirms Seth's opinion that "George belongs to this town" (107), because George's ideal of being a writer is as devoid of meaning as any other social title: he speaks of writers traveling the world, being their own boss, and tossing off words to get by. And yet, just before Seth's arrival, we are told that George "had been sitting for an hour idly playing with a lead pencil" (104–5). And in his monologue George unwittingly spells out to Seth a simplistic and shallow theory of writing, saying that he must fall in love with Helen White in order to write a love story. Seth recognizes that his so-called "comrade" is no different from "the men of the town who were . . . perpetually talking of nothing" (105), and he leaves in a huff.

Throughout the story Seth seems to be a fairly acute observer of how words are duplicitous and, accordingly, of how social roles lack substance. But in dismissing the signification of language and social forms, he can find no workable, nonverbal alternative. This point becomes clear when, determined to leave town and immerse himself in work, he seeks out Helen White, who, we are told, has had a long-standing crush on him. Given an opportunity to find a sympathetic person eager to understand him (unlike George, who was so preoccupied with himself), Seth nevertheless allows himself to get swept up with words, as so many other characters in the story do. The irony is impossible to miss, as when Seth complains to Helen that "everyone talks and talks," while he himself is swept up with ideas that he must seek work "where talk don't count" (111), thus negating the chance for "some vague adventure [with Helen] that had been present in the spirit of the night." Helen summarily dismisses him, advising him to "go and talk with your mother." Instead of realizing his missed opportunity, Seth merely reverts to his knee-jerk belief that he will never find love because that is reserved for people who talk a lot. Preoccupied with the meaninglessness of words, Seth succumbs to spouting empty bromides himself at a crucial moment. He knows no other way to transcend verbal communication.

The narrator, throughout this tale, constantly underscores the inadequacy of spoken and written communication, sometimes employing almost playful humor in the process. Early on, when she reassures Seth that his father was a good man, Virginia tells her son that Clarence Richmond "should not have tried to be a man of affairs," no doubt missing the unintended pun (100). When she must find work after her husband's death, Virginia becomes a court stenographer, a position dealing with the precise replication of words, a job that lacks any originality or creativity. When a younger Seth runs away from home, Virginia is so determined to express her feelings to her son that "she got out pencil and paper and wrote down a series of sharp, stinging reproofs she intended to pour out upon him" (102). But once he returns, she is unable to read from her script. George Willard rhapsodizes about writing but has nothing to show for it in this tale. Helen White's admiring notes to Seth also seem to have been shallow and formulaic because, the narrator tells us, the notes "reflected a mind inflamed by novel reading" (108). And, of course, Seth's own sudden loquaciousness with Helen dispels any potential the two had for meaningful understanding. Words fail in every effort to communicate meaning.

Nearly every social role pertaining to work also seems severed from substance in the tale. Clarence Richmond's career proved not to be as impressive as everyone thought; Virginia Richmond's job ironically entails transcribing other people's words; Tom Willard wiles away the time debating with his guests instead of attending to the upkeep of the floundering hotel; George Willard is a reporter and aspiring writer who does little in this story except talk about a writing career; and even "half-witted" Turk Smollet, whom Seth watches transporting a wheelbarrow full of boards, purposely goes out of his way to traverse Main Street only to "exhibit his skill in wheeling the boards" (107). The only significant evidence of work in the story is a crumbling artifact of someone's past employment, the Richmond house that was built with limestone from

Seth's grandfather's quarry. And this edifice, the narrator mentions, formerly "the show place of the town . . . was said in the village to have become run down," supplanted in town pride by Banker White's new house. And yet, as his distrust of language did not prevent him from being infected with it in his exchange with Helen, so too does Seth's distrust of social roles not prevent him from obsessing over the need to work. After his failed talk with George, Seth becomes fixated with the idea of busying himself with work. The idea looms so great in his mind that it even warps his dreams: he imagines himself and Helen White nuzzled in a romantic, pastoral setting outside of town; but in the dream he chooses not to become intimate with her, preferring instead to listen to an "army of bees that sang the sustained masterful song of labor above his head" (110)! At the end of the tale, Seth remains in a psychological stasis, rightly suspecting and yet succumbing nonetheless to the inefficacies of both language and social roles. He can neither communicate nor act in any manner that deviates from the conventional behavior of the town.

In "Hands," the narrator reinforces the notion that Wing lives his frustrating life in Winesburg as a penance for past transgressions by concluding the tale with Wing on his knees picking up crumbs off the floor "like a devotee going swiftly through decade after decade of his rosary" (17). Anderson's emphasis in this story is on the town's powerful ability to subject an individual to its scrutiny and summary judgment and the consequences of that subjection. In "'Queer,'" he depicts the opposite dynamic: in Elmer Cowley we see a character who willfully subjects himself to self-scrutiny and self-condemnation, in the midst of a community that seems at best indifferent to his presence in town. Elmer is very much akin to Foucault's conception of the insane who subject themselves to what they believe is normalized morality because they think they may—or may not—be under society's observation.

Elmer's paranoia centers on the uneasy transition his family makes from the farm to the town. As he tells Mook about his former farm, "When we lived out here it was different" (161). Living there in relative seclusion, Elmer did not have to situate himself in what he later convinces himself to be a competitive, judgmental town. But once the family settles in town, Elmer becomes a paranoid, in large part because of his father's failure to run a store. Ebenezer Cowley, we are told, is a figure cut adrift from both farm and town: "As a merchant Ebenezer was not happily placed in life and he had not been happily placed as a farmer. Still he existed" (156). As a merchant, Ebenezer is a failure: his store, situated off the high-trafficked Main Street, is filled with wares that no one buys. Ebenezer succumbs to every pitch of traveling sales-men, who peddle ostensibly cutting-edge goods that people will be attracted to purchase. However, as the narrator relates, objects like molding honey-combs remained for sale, as do also "the coat hangers, patent suspender but-tons, cans of roof paint, bottles of rheumatism cure and a substitute for coffee that companioned the honey in its patient willingness to serve the public" (156). And Ebenezer himself is an apparent eyesore, appearing everyday "un-washed" in a worn, greasy Prince Albert coat. To Elmer, then, his father's di-sheveled appearance and pathetic business contribute to his own paranoia. In a culture that values success and looking sharp, Elmer simply projects these characteristics upon the town; he convinces himself that because of his family's failures the town must therefore regard him and his father as queer.

The only critical judgment spoken against Elmer in the entire story comes from a salesman who quite appropriately shouts, "Crazy, that's what he is—crazy!" after Elmer threatens him with a gun (157). Such judgment is hardly representative of the town, however, because as a "Jewish traveling salesman," the salesman would probably be someone whom the town would deem queer. It is Elmer himself who fills the tale with his fears of being singled out for ridicule. From the opening scene, when he thinks George Willard is watching him clumsily replace his shoelaces, Elmer believes that the entire town is view-ing and judging him. To Elmer, George "typified the town, represented in his person the spirit of the town. . . . Did he not represent public opinion and had not the public opinion of Winesburg condemned the Cowleys to queerness?" (158–59). That George was also sporting a "new overcoat and looked very spruce and dressed up" (162), in dramatic contrast to his father's ratty attire, no doubt contributes to Elmer's paranoid feelings toward George in particular.

Ironically, Elmer seems to wish for little more than to be just another face in the crowd, to blend seamlessly into the social fabric. For instance, after he chases away the salesman, he declares, "I will not be queer—one to be looked at and listened to" (158). He confesses to his half-witted friend Mook, "Even the clothes mother used to wear were not like other people's clothes" (160). His goal in leaving Winesburg is to settle in Cleveland, where he "would lose himself in the crowds there. . . . Gradually he would become like other men and would be indistinguishable" (163). Elmer leaves himself only two outlooks: to be another face in the crowd or to stand out, which to him means being queer.

With these static alternatives fixed in his mind, Elmer nevertheless attempts to gain an understanding with others through verbal communication; but all

57

such attempts are failures. After the incident with the salesman, Elmer turns to his father, "waiting for some word of understanding from [him]," and receives only the garbled "expression regarding being 'laundered'" in reply. With Mook he "talked earnestly and with great freedom," no doubt because he is in the company of one who he knows will not judge him queer; however, he realizes that the potential for understanding is futile with the "half-witted old fellow." And with George Willard he twice fails to "declare his determination not to be queer" (162). Of course, in striving so consciously not to be queer, Elmer behaves in such a way that anyone in town would think him so—if anyone were interested. Fixated with the need not to be queer, and unable to articulate this need, Elmer relies on nonverbal means. But, like Beaut McGregor in *Marching Men*, Elmer resorts to physical force to communicate in lieu of language. He threatens the salesman with violence; he yearns to strike at the "greater enemy" of the town by striking at George (159); he "tried to talk and his arms began to pump up and down," in his first confrontation with George, groping for expression that would not come; and finally, at the train station, he "danced with fury" after uttering the line about being "washed and ironed and starched" before resorting to actual blows against the reporter. In uttering the pointless expression, Elmer unwittingly underscores the vacancy of meaning in language, while nonetheless allowing himself to remain obsessed with the articulated concept of being queer.

Subjecting himself to his own rigid scrutiny of what normal, accepted behavior should be, Elmer isolates himself without the intervention of the town. His repeating of Mook's meaningless expression only reinforces his self-fulfilling paranoia of perceiving himself as queer. Apparently nobody else in town is aware that Mook coined the term; the expression, like his own behavior, is invested with dubious meaning only by Elmer himself. But because Elmer is so convinced that his behavior is aberrant in the eyes of the town, the town indirectly functions as a controlling force; Elmer, like Foucault's depiction of the insane, feels compelled to exert self-surveillance and self-judgment.

These stories focus more closely than the other *Winesburg* tales on the grotesques' direct interactions with the town. Some stories, like "Hands," "A Man of Ideas," and "The Thinker," display the town's overt influence on the grotesques; others, like "The Philosopher" and "'Queer,'" show how controlling a force the town can be even when it does not directly interfere in a character's life. Whether it directly molds a character's identity or serves as an unseen arbiter, the town permeates these characters' identities. What augments this frustrating situation is that the normalized standards that the town embodies and that the grotesques respond to are generally devoid of constructive meaning: in each of these tales, Anderson shows how the language that gives expression to such standards is typically manipulated in order to reinforce the town's authority while undermining and otherwise subjugating the autonomous identity of the grotesques. Rather than serving as a means of understanding, language instead functions as another disciplinary tool for the various forces in the town that wield control. In harmonious fashion, Anderson's very narration of these and the other tales reaffirms the instability of language; it refuses to give us a seamless, truthful tale, and as a result, it devalues its own authority as it acknowledges the reader's own subjective participation. Anderson interweaves these various threads throughout the book.

. . .

We can find such strands in other tales as well, such as those that concern people who mold their lives according to formulaic prescriptions, many of which emerge from the nation's popular mythology. These tales do not necessarily dwell upon the interplay between the individual and some segment of the town; in fact, most of the individuals' predicaments in these tales were grounded in experiences that took place outside of Winesburg. Alice Hindman's acknowledgment to herself—that "many people must live and die alone, *even in Winesburg*" (92, emphasis mine)—forces readers to remember that experiences that transform individuals into grotesques can and do occur anywhere, in both urban and rural locales. Anderson crafts several tales in the book around characters whose momentous experiences concerning grotesqueness took place elsewhere. In suggesting how grotesqueness is endemic to the wider American culture, Anderson also draws our attention to the power that popular cultural myths—as well as any prescriptive bromides instructing one on how to live one's life—have in influencing one's identity. Just as Sam McPherson became obsessed with the national success myth in the little corn town of Caxton in *Windy McPherson's Son*, so too do characters in the *Winesburg* tales display a similar tendency to realign their lives according to abstract formulas that fail when applied to the vicissitudes of everyday life. Recalling "The Book of the Grotesque," we can understand why they are bound to fail: they may indeed be beautiful concepts in the abstract, but as formulaic verbal constructs they are inherently inadequate as vessels of all-inclusive meaning. As static ideals, often reduced to pithy catchphrases, they may function as imprecise guides to living

59

in society, but because they are devoid of comprehensive meaning, they are also deceptive and injurious to anyone who wholly subscribes to them. Postmodern concerns with language and the subjection of the individual are also on display in these tales that focus on characters who embrace larger cultural nostrums too literally.

"Respectability" is one such case in point. Wash Williams, described by the narrator as like a "huge, grotesque kind of monkey" in a zoo (93), is "the ugliest thing in town." The formative experience of his grotesqueness, however, occurred years earlier outside of Winesburg when he was married and rising up the social ladder. As the title of the story suggests, "Respectability" provides us with a character who embraced the popular myth of rising up in the world and then faced a crushing disappointment when the superficial ideal did not mirror his own experience.

As he relates his story to George Willard, in marrying the blonde, blue-eyed daughter of a local Dayton dentist and then acquiring both a job promotion and a new house, Wash succeeded in collecting the material tokens of respectability. Ensconced in urban Columbus in his new position as telegraph dispatcher, Wash "settled down with his young wife and began buying a house on the installment plan" (96). In following the prescriptive formula for achieving respectability, he seemed well on his way toward solidifying the clichéd picture of having wife, house with white picket fence, and commensurate number of children. What he does not adequately deal with, though—and what the myth gives no mention of—is the subject of sex and other intimate relations that occur between husband and wife.

Concerning these subjects, the narrator informs us, Wash practiced an undeviating, mechanical routine: "With a kind of religious fervor he had managed to go through the pitfalls of youth and to remain virginal until after his marriage" (97). For Wash, sex is something to be regulated and kept distinct from his unfettered portrait of respectability. The narrator may tell us that Wash "made for George Willard a picture of his life in the house at Columbus, Ohio with the young wife," but the only thing that Wash dwells on for the reporter is a highly ritualistic and rather sterile description of his planting seeds in his garden. With glaringly sexual overtones, Wash relates how his wife would stand apart from him, handing him seeds from a bag, "that I might thrust them into the warm, soft ground" (97). He would then crawl on the ground to her and kiss her feet and ankles, and he deemed it a kind of ecstasy when "the hem of her garment touched [his] face." Such actions are all externalized, artificial forms of sexuality; they remain once removed from actual sexual intimacy between marriage partners, no doubt because matters regarding sex would not have been found in any version of the success myth. Accordingly, marriage remains for Wash a static, sanitized ideal.

His wife's infidelity became a jarring moment of realization for Wash: suddenly feeling betrayed by the success myth, he rejected the superficial props of the myth, sending his wife back to her mother, withdrawing all his savings to give to her, and eventually selling his house to give her all the proceeds. Recognizing a wide gulf between the hollow ideal of the myth and his own experience, Wash endured another crushing blow to his ideal when his wife's mother invited him to her home. The home, he tells George, was a model of respectability, and the family "were what is called respectable people" (98). Craving to "forgive and forget," Wash remained unchanged in his attitudes toward marital intimacy, however, because he tells George that he would have "faint[ed] away" had his wife only touched him with her hand. Still holding on to his sterile beliefs of intimacy, Wash's conception of respectability was forever quashed when the mother presented her daughter naked to him. Alienated from the ideology of success, betrayed even by his staid notions of sex, Wash becomes in Winesburg a physical and psychological grotesque, where "everything about him was unclean" (93).

An isolated, misogynistic figure, Wash nevertheless is occasionally respected by the town, as the narrator relates. Like the pathetic carpenter in "The Book of the Grotesque" who, the narrator reminds us, was still a "lovable" character, Wash, too, is endowed with a kind of "perverted beauty": "Here and there a man respected the operator. Instinctively the man felt in him a glowing resentment of something he had not the courage to resent" (94). Indeed, Wash does have a conscious awareness that the hallowed ideals that so many try to follow are void of substance, and it is perhaps his brusqueness and utter disregard of social niceties, which are the results of such awareness, that prompt the respect of some of his peers. However astute his disgust with society may be, though, Wash remains a static, ineffectual individual, his entire personality frozen in time from the moment his wife cheated on him years earlier. Fixed in his misogynistic worldview, he offers himself no opportunity to move beyond that past experience, which he allowed to permanently shape his identity. That is why he tells his tale to George Willard—not to attain some understanding for himself but to reaffirm his rigid beliefs and "destroy" any dreams George may have of achieving any kind of intimacy with another person.

61

If "Respectability" offers a retrospective look at how an individual long ago forged his identity around static ideals, then "Tandy" provides an eyewitness account for the reader of how a person may be initially attracted to such ideals. Nearly universally regarded by Anderson scholars as the weakest tale in the book, "Tandy" does provide a fleeting, though underdeveloped, glimpse at what motivates someone to be drawn to a static ideal: the need to believe in something that has the semblance of a definitive purpose in an otherwise discouraging world. As Judith Arcana has pointed out, "Tandy" is a unique tale in the collection, depicting someone who evidently passes his own static truth on to another.[7]

The drunken stranger from Cleveland who bestows the name Tandy on the child is a direct antidote to the child's father, Tom Hard, and this may clarify in part why the child eventually fixates on his ideal. In explaining his alcoholic addiction, the stranger tells the father that he has "not lost faith" in his ideal conception of women; in contrast, the father, we are told, "proclaimed himself an agnostic and was so absorbed in destroying the ideas of God . . . that he never saw God manifesting himself in the little child" (113). The child, "half forgotten" by her father, whose name the narrator does not even bother to disclose, survives "here and there on the bounty of her dead mother's relatives," living in physical and spiritual squalor. The stranger essentially instills in the child a life-affirming belief in herself, a psychological life preserver that satisfies her need to believe in something purposeful.

The stranger invests the name Tandy with his definition of the ideal woman, emphasizing that this "new quality in woman" involves the strength to endure struggles and defeats. Addressing the child directly, the stranger tells her, "Dare to be strong and courageous. That is the road. Venture anything. Be brave enough to dare to be loved" (115). It is not surprising that a child immersed in an atmosphere of doubt and defeat would embrace such words, as the girl demonstrates when she pleads with her father to be called Tandy. The words of the stranger serve as both a balm and a tonic; they seem to console her while at the same time energizing her.

The narrator tells us that the stranger "gave a name rich with meaning to Tom Hard's daughter" (113), and later the stranger tells the child, "I understand. . . . Perhaps of all men I alone understand" (115). Herein lie a few problems. As nearly every other tale in the book illustrates, people become grotesques when they consciously shape their lives around prescriptive ideals; furthermore, when they later attempt to communicate their frustrated stories to another, in search of understanding, they invariably fail because they rely on language as the means of achieving that understanding. Both the experiences of the characters and the style of narration constantly undermine the efficacy of language; in fact, language is often complicit in a character's becoming grotesque. In effect, then, when she claims Tandy as a name, the child seems to join the long procession of figures who snatch up truths in the old man's dream in "The Book of the Grotesque." Like George Willard in "The Philosopher," the girl's youthful naïveté makes her gullible, vulnerable to a suspect character's pearls of wisdom. Perhaps, too, Anderson shows how readers may be lured by the stranger's earnest pleas into a false sense that all will be well.[8] However enticing and reassuring the stranger's ideal may be and however assured his claim of understanding the girl, the story nevertheless provides the scenario of a grotesque in the making.

In "Tandy" we encounter someone who chooses to mold her identity based on another's ideal. But in "Loneliness," Anderson presents us with a character who, in some ways like Seth Richmond, remains in a condition of psychological stasis that prevents him from forging *any* social identity. Enoch Robinson, the "little wrinkled man-boy" (144), is a figure who as an adult prefers the childish world of his imagination in part because he can find no viable entrée into the world of adults. Neither his paintings nor his verbal communications afford him such a means; as a result, Enoch peoples a world of his own fancy. The narration in this tale, too, underscores Enoch's incapacity to communicate for himself, as is seen in the repeated intrusions of the narrator. But although the narrator seems to come to Enoch's aid, in "speaking" on his behalf, he also draws attention to his own unreliability in communicating the "facts" and the thoughts of Enoch's life. In "Loneliness" we have another rich melding of postmodern concerns in both the content and the telling of the tale.

Enoch's displacement from society begins in his childhood, which was spent on a farm two miles outside of Winesburg. Like Seth, Enoch as a young boy was accepted by the town largely because he was a quiet figure: "Old citizens remembered him as a quiet, smiling youth inclined to silence" (135). In New York to study art, Enoch seemed to have all the superficial means within reach to become an artist, but, in a long aside, the narrator explains why he never did:

Nothing ever turned out for Enoch Robinson. He could draw well enough and he had many odd delicate thoughts hidden away in his brain that might have expressed themselves through the brush of a painter, but he was always

63

a child and that was a handicap to his worldly development. He never grew up and of course he couldn't understand people and he couldn't make people understand him. (135)

Here, as elsewhere in the tale, we have things explained to us almost too neatly. Anderson very cleverly magnifies the narrator's authoritative presence in this tale to emphasize Enoch's incapacity to express himself.

This incapacity is evident when the narrator describes Enoch's apartment in New York: "On the walls were pictures he had made, crude things, half finished." His friends—"artists of the kind that talk. Everyone knows of the talking artists"—fill the room with meaningless jargon about painting. "Words were said," the narrator reports, "about line and values and composition, lots of words, such as are always being said" (136). Enoch is excited to enter into the conversation, to explain his paintings: "He knew what he wanted to say, but he knew also that he could never by any possibility say it." As if to prove this statement, the narrator furnishes us with a detailed explanation of one of Enoch's paintings, which itself seems to elude meaning, emphasizing that the explanation is the "kind of thing young Enoch Robinson trembled to say . . . , but he always ended by saying nothing" (137–38). The entire description, we are reminded, is at best the *narrator's* approximation of Enoch's thoughts. Enoch's own identity remains as elusive as the meaning of his painting.

From this frustrated attempt to be an expressive artist among his peers, Enoch then creates his own imaginary world, a place where he can be finally "self-confident and bold." The figures who inhabit this world are similar to those who filled the old man's dreams in "The Book of the Grotesque," for they are all spirits of people Enoch knew back in Winesburg. Unlike the old man, though, Enoch has no interest in them except to use them as "people with whom he could really talk, people he could harangue and scold by the hour, servants, you see, to his fancy" (138). Rejecting the physical world and the uncertainty of knowing actual people, Enoch becomes a "kind of tiny blue-eyed king" in his Washington Square flat, which he inhabits with his imaginary people.

However, after he feels lonely from such isolation, Enoch reenters the physical world, this time not as an artist but as a participant in the myth of success. Securing a wife and children and working as an advertising illustrator, he now "play[s] at a new game": "For a while he was very proud of himself in the role of producing citizen of the world" (139). Finding no voice as an artist, he eventually fails as a "producing citizen" also. Painting at least afforded him the chance to express something of himself; as a professional solid citizen, though, he is merely playing a "role" in a "game." Consequently, while feeling "choked and walled in by the life in the apartment," Enoch is released by this lifestyle after his mother dies and leaves him a tidy inheritance. Like Wash Williams after his separation from his wife, Enoch no longer has any interest in the material props of the myth of success: he leaves his wife and children and takes up his old flat, where he is again among "the people of his fancy, playing with them, talking to them, happy as a child is happy" (140).

His return to his imaginary world is short-lived, though: the narrator insistently mentions that "something happened. Of course something did happen. . . . He was too happy. Something had to come into his world. Something had to drive him out of the New York room to live out his life, an obscure, jerky little figure" (140). As before, the narrator here seems too solicitous about providing a neat explanation, as he is also when describing the setting in which Enoch tries to make George Willard understand what happened in New York. After Enoch tells George, "You'll understand if you try hard enough," the narrator makes clear that in their conversation Enoch "came to the vital thing, the story of the woman and of what drove him out of the city to live out his life alone and defeated in Winesburg" (142). In having the narrator be an overtly authoritative presence in the story, Anderson underscores Enoch's inability to communicate. In effect, the narrator becomes another figure who, like the chatty artists, stifles opportunities for Enoch to express himself.

Enoch's epiphanic moment in New York occurs when he is attracted to a woman who becomes a regular visitor to his room. Contrary to the narrator's version of events, Enoch in New York was already "alone and defeated." He is sexually drawn to the woman while also repelled by her, because she "was so grown up, you see. She was a woman. I thought she would be bigger than I was there in the room" (143). After Enoch tells her about his imaginary people and "everything that meant anything to [him]," he knows that he is risking the surrender of his imaginary world—with the possible gain, though, of a genuine, understanding relationship with someone. But having had no such experience before, Enoch does not know how to react when he thinks the woman understands him; he becomes hysterical, chasing her out of the apartment as a result. The "child-mind" of Enoch cannot fathom how to live without having the refuge of that imaginary world. As he tells George, "I wanted her to understand but, don't you see, I couldn't let her understand. I felt that then she would know everything, that I would be submerged, drowned out, you see" (143).

The narrator refers to the childishness of Enoch throughout the tale and particularly stresses it in contrasting Enoch with George. George is described in this tale as a youth, not a child, a "growing boy" full of "youthful sadness" (140). For Anderson, youth and youthfulness are positive attributes; not necessarily denoting chronological age, the terms suggest an innocence of sorts and a receptivity to understanding. They are used this way in the introductory tale, "The Book of the Grotesque," as well as in the penultimate story, "Sophistication." In contrast, Enoch is described as childlike throughout "Loneliness." In the story's opening, the narrator states that "the child in him kept bumping into things" (135), and Enoch himself seems to confirm this observation in the story's conclusion when he tells George, "Things went to smash" (144). Desirous of achieving understanding with human society, Enoch remains in a psychological limbo because he has no means of achieving that understanding: art and language are for him elusive means of expression. Therefore, without the ability to integrate himself into society, Enoch hovers somewhere between his imaginary world and the actual world, where he feels "submerged" and "drowned." And when Enoch tells George, "but now I'm all alone" in the last line of the tale, the narrator too, who was so outspoken throughout, accentuates the sentiment with his silence.

In "Drink," Tom Foster is similar to Seth Richmond in being accepted by society even though he is segregated from it. Tom, who was raised by his grandmother under harsh conditions in Cincinnati, is a character apparently so traumatized by his upbringing that he is emotionally paralyzed, unable to interact with others. Throughout the tale the narrator presents Tom as someone who makes highly controlled and limited excursions into society; wary of either experiencing further pain or inflicting it on others, he constructs isolated incidents of interacting and then withdraws into the safer confines of his mind. Unlike Enoch Robinson, though, Tom seems to have no alternative existence to withdraw to.

As a child in Cincinnati, Tom had to endure a grueling life in the more sordid part of the city. Both of his parents died young, and Tom was left to his grandmother, who had become a "half worn-out old woman worker" after having been formerly a "strong, capable little old thing" (172). Tom "ran about with tough boys" and was exposed to a steady stream of prostitution, drunkenness, fights, and crime. What allowed him to survive in this environment, the narrator tells us, was that he "never asserted himself. That was one thing that helped him escape" (174). This is not exactly true, however. A silent but genial personality, Tom in his early years made isolated and defined attempts to immerse himself in his surroundings, first by stealing, and then by visiting a prostitute. As he explained his stealing to his grandmother, "It is all right to be ashamed and makes me understand new things" (174). And concerning his apparently unconsummated experience with a prostitute, the narrator says that "after that one experience . . . he dismissed women from his mind" (177).

This pattern of controlled interaction and subsequent withdrawal continues when Tom and his grandmother move to Winesburg. A native of Winesburg, the grandmother jumps at the chance to return when she finds a pocketbook containing cash. Anticipating that the small town will provide a wholesome environment, she is upset to find that "the tiny village of fifty years before had grown into a thriving town in her absence" (173). Nevertheless, Tom "enjoyed life in Winesburg," the narrator tells us (175), getting by by doing odd jobs and otherwise loafing. "In Winesburg, among its citizens he had always the power to be a part of and yet distinctly apart from the life about him." In his silent way, Tom ingratiates himself with the town by being an innocuous presence. He indulges his basic senses, as when he sits for an hour in Hern's grocery inhaling the "rich odor" of coffee being ground; this indulgence is contrasted to his experience with the prostitute in her room, the smell of which "he never forgot" (176).

After two years of such an inoffensive existence, Tom again feels the urge to experiment with interacting with his peers. Influenced by his fellow teenagers who are actively dating, Tom falls in love with Helen White. The narrator states that this was a "problem" for Tom but that he "settled it in his own way": "He had a fight, a quiet determined little fight of his own, to keep his desires in the channel where he thought they belonged, but on the whole he was victorious" (177). From his previous experiences in Cincinnati, Tom seems convinced that any emotional attachment is unhealthy; hence, he gets drunk for the first time for the sole purpose of dreaming about Helen, rather than seeking any meeting with her. Ironically, he does find an opportunity to share his thoughts, but only after a solicitous George Willard pulls him into the *Winesburg Eagle* office.

George in this scene displays contrary emotions: he assists Tom with "motherly solicitude," even moving him outside when he fears that Tom might get sick inside the newspaper office; but he also is jealous and defensive with Tom when he starts sharing his fantasies about Helen. The result is that George squelches an opportunity for Tom to achieve understanding. After George scolds him, we are told that Tom "couldn't quarrel with George Willard because he

67

was incapable of quarreling, so he got up to go away" (180). We know that in his sobering condition Tom is desirous of finding understanding, because he repeats several times the lines "You see how it is"; "Don't you see how it is?"; and "Don't you understand?" (179, 180).

In spite of George's efforts to silence him, Tom does share some revealing thoughts, which do more to enlighten the reader than to gain George's understanding. He tells George, "I wanted to suffer, to be hurt somehow. I thought that was what I should do. I wanted to suffer, you see, because everyone suffers and does wrong. I thought of a lot of things to do, but they wouldn't work. They all hurt some one else" (180). To Tom, any meaningful interaction with others is fraught with hurt and disappointment. Thus, to preclude hurting Helen White, Tom gets drunk and then says, "It hurt me to do what I did and made everything strange. That's why I did it." In essence, Tom wills his own isolation and subjection in society, because experience has taught him that only pain results from interacting with others. He convinced himself that such was the case in Cincinnati, and he does so again in Winesburg.

In "Respectability," "Tandy," "Loneliness," and "Drink," Anderson makes it clear that the condition of the modern grotesque is hardly unique to small-town America. Characters in these tales experience both external pressures to succumb to prescriptive formulas of behavior and pressures from within themselves, resembling, in essence, many of Foucault's insane or criminals. Their actions result in a psychological and spiritual isolation from both the wider urban landscape and the narrower confines of Winesburg. As Stephen Enniss has stated, "Clearly the tragedies of Anderson's *Winesburg, Ohio* are not unique to Winesburg, but are instead common human tragedies that can appear in any community."[9] Furthermore, as with the other grouping of tales discussed earlier, language, the very basis of meaning, communication, and understanding, is found wanting and is often, in fact, the very instrument of the grotesques' isolation. But in the broad canvas of *Winesburg,* Anderson also provides portraits of characters who suffer from obsessions with solitary truths, such as those involving religion and sexual relationships. Let us first examine those tales in which religion is the primary obsession.

.   .   .

Religion, whether the actual rituals of a particular faith or simply a general consciousness of conventionally pious behavior, becomes a focal point in several of the *Winesburg* tales. Anderson wisely avoids entering into theological exegeses; what more concerns him is the influence organized religion has on certain individuals, especially how individuals adapt or outright manipulate religious dogma or rituals to buffer their actions. In several of his tales, however, such adaptations are not presented as one's attempt to validate one's behavior through willful deceit. As Jesse Bentley in several of the "Godliness" stories and Curtis Hartman in "The Strength of God" illustrate, religious precepts mold these characters' actions as much as they themselves are compelled to interpret such precepts to validate their behavior. These characters convince themselves that as decent, God-fearing men they are acting sincerely in accordance with scriptural truths. Wrapping themselves within the mantle of God's truth allows them to rationalize actions that are sometimes quite contrary to Christian tenets. Why they can rationalize actions that seem to belie Judeo-Christian dogma has much to do with the malleability of language: Jesse and Curtis actively demonstrate the unreliability of meaning in language whenever they creatively (and subjectively) interpret the Word. But as Anderson shows throughout the book, a blind embrace of prescriptive truths—including those interpreted from the Bible—results in failure and frustration. Superficially these characters appear to the public as successful and respected men, perhaps in large part because they project the aura that God is indeed working through them; however, as Anderson shows us, behind these thin veneers the two men are psychological wrecks, ironically because they so desperately need to believe that they are instruments of God.

In the first two parts of "Godliness" and in "Terror," Jesse Bentley convinces himself that he is acting as a typological incarnation of the biblical Jesse. In the process of expanding his father's farm, he convinces himself, "It is God's work I have come to the land to do" (48). He further convinces himself that all the neighboring farmers are potential enemies—enemies only of himself, though he widens the scope of their threat to include God also: "Into Jesse's mind came the conviction that all of the Ohio farmers who owned land in the valley of Wine Creek were Philistines and enemies of God" (50). Through a "fantastic impulse, half fear, half greediness," Jesse entreats God to have his wife deliver him a son, so that a Bentley dynasty might be launched, a dynasty that would fortify his expanding position of power. The narrator's admission that Jesse's motivation for such a wish is influenced by greed, however, is revealing. In essence, Jesse Bentley adapts Old Testament models to validate a rapacious need on his part to assert power and command respect, neither of which he enjoyed before he returned home from Bible school to run the farm.

The narrator approvingly summarizes the early years of the Bentleys' experience in the Midwest. After years of "long hard labor" in clearing the land for farming, the Bentleys continued to work like "driven animals." In sum, "Into their lives came little that was not coarse and brutal and outwardly they were themselves coarse and brutal" (43). However difficult such a life was, the narrator says, early settlers of the Midwest, like the Bentleys, had innate, redeeming values nonetheless: they possessed an "animal-like poetic fervor" (43), and "much of the old brutal ignorance . . . had in it also a kind of beautiful childlike innocence" (49). These qualities were apparently absent in the young Jesse, who was deemed an "odd sheep" (45).

The narrator presents Jesse as a conspicuous modification of these early settlers. For four years he had been away at school, studying to "become a scholar and eventually to become a minister" (44). When he returns home to take control of the farm, his neighbors and "the nearby town of Winesburg" lightly dismiss him because they believe him to lack the virile qualities of his father and brothers: "By the standards of his day Jesse did not look like a man at all. He was small and very slender and womanish of body" (45). Doubtless sensing his neighbors' dismissal of him, Jesse resorts to his biblical studies to help him "think of himself as an extraordinary man, one set apart from his fellows" (47). To validate this opinion of himself, he asks for God's intercession, "Create in me another Jesse, like that one of old, to rule over men and to be the father of sons who shall be rulers!" (48). In the process of expanding his farm he becomes "avaricious" and "impatient"; he feels that as the "true servant of God the entire stretch of country . . . should have come into his possession" (50). In effect, as Jesse's character is in part molded by a culture that "believed in God and in God's power to control [people's] lives" (49), it is also significantly shaped by his own manipulation of that very Bible-centered culture.

As Jesse's tale continues in the second part of "Godliness," set many years later after Jesse's entreaty for a male heir went unanswered, we find that the farmer has become a psychological victim of his self-conscious attempt to be God's agent. In spite of being the most powerful farmer in the valley—"there were few farms in the valley that did not belong to him" (56)—Jesse is a "bitterly disappointed man," until his grandson David comes to live on the farm. The "old thing" in him to be a "man of God and a leader among men of God" was still in him, we are told, but such an ostensible goal seems to have been long supplanted by his now greater desire—the "greedy thing in him"—to "make money faster than it could be made by tilling the land" (57). If his will to exert power and command respect had earlier been cloaked by religious fanaticism, at some point in the intervening years since Jesse allowed himself to be swept up by the then-current notions of utilizing industrialism to reap greater and quicker monetary rewards. His delusion of being God's agent is replaced by an undisguised zeal for mammon, an obsession that the unusually informative narrator prepared us for in the first part of the tale.

In the earlier section, the narrator provides a didactic screed against "the coming of industrialism" and the media's role in contributing to its growth. The modern-day farmer, we are told, "has his mind filled to overflowing with the words of other men," as they are found in newspapers and magazines, with the result that "the farmer by the stove is brother to the men of the cities" (49). This modern-day farmer, now filled with ideas of industrialism and making money, has replaced the (genuinely?) God-centered farmer of a former generation. Jesse, we are informed in the second section, evolves into the modern farmer:

> The beginning of the most materialistic age in the history of the world, when wars would be fought without patriotism, when men would forget God and only pay attention to moral standards, when the will to power would replace the will to serve and beauty would be well-nigh forgotten in the terrible headlong rush of mankind toward the acquiring of possessions, was telling its story to Jesse the man of God as it was to the men about him. (57)

As Jesse realizes, "it was harder to get back the old feeling of a close and personal God who lived in the sky overhead and who might at any moment . . . appoint for him some heroic task to be done" (57).

When David moves into his house, Jesse renews the "dreams" of his pious youth that he be a powerful agent of God. Apparently such dreams had been muted as he became the most important farmer in the valley, the immediate effects of his material wealth distracting him from his more spiritual aims. The narrator makes it crystal clear, though, that such a distraction has had physical and no doubt psychological repercussions for Jesse: at the time when the second section commences, we are told that although he is fifty-five years of age, he "looked seventy and was worn out with much thinking and scheming" (56), and when he talks, his left eye twitches (57). Having once deluded himself with his personalized sense of piety, Jesse revisits the subject soon after David's arrival—except that now, as a man long used to achieving his

71

material goals, he expects God to become a solicitous agent to his plans. Late in the story, allowing his "dreams [to] take entire possession of him" (59), Jesse takes David to the woods and commands God to manifest himself to him: "Make a sign to me, God. . . . Here I stand with the boy David. Come down to me out of the sky and make Thy presence known to me" (61).

It is interesting that Anderson uses the word "dreams" to characterize Jesse's renewed obsession, for in most of the other *Winesburg* tales, he regards dreams as potentially positive agents in the formation of one's character. Here, though, they assume negative connotations, primarily because Jesse attempts to actualize his old dreams with perfect precision. As his literal adaptation of the machine-age creed makes him a grotesque, so too does his literal application of his messianic old dreams. The ensuing scene in the woods with David, wherein Jesse beckons God to give him a sign, proves disastrous for Jesse. And as "Terror," the fourth part of the tale, illustrates, a similar scene in the woods with his grandson will have even more dramatic consequences.

In this brief sketch, the narrator again says that Jesse's continuing material prosperity coalesces with his renewed religious zeal. Roughly three years pass between the second and last sections, and during this time Jesse's power and wealth increase exponentially. While wallowing in an "exultant" state from a recent successful venture, Jesse again turns his thoughts to forcing God's hand to give both his grandson and him a sign. Desirous that the "glory of God [be] made manifest" to David, in order to "make a true man of God of him also" (74), Jesse decides to take his fifteen-year-old grandson back to the woods, this time to offer God the sacrifice of a lamb, an act that frightens the boy. Full of trepidation, the boy uses a slingshot to strike his knife-wielding grandfather; thinking that he has "killed the man of God," David flees the region, never to return (75). The overt moral, as Jesse later relates it, is that he "was too greedy for glory" (76). Thus, Jesse's twofold obsession of being a man of God and a powerful farmer who commands the respect of his peers ends in failure: he literally becomes the Goliath-like figure whom he had long ago feared could "defeat" him (50), and he denounces his hubris and greediness—greediness not only for glory but apparently also for an excessive power associated with it. But what deflates his denunciation is the context that Jesse creates for it, in which he still holds on to his fixation that God show him a sign. Jesse misses the irony, which he unwittingly provides, that "a messenger from God had taken the boy" (76).

Perhaps Anderson intended the three parts of "Godliness" that center on Jesse to be an ironic parable of sorts, but it seems evident that, just as Jesse's obsessions become frustrated from the scripted applications of his dreams, so too this tale suffers from a literal application of Jesse's moral. Along with "Tandy," "Godliness" is too reminiscent of the didactic heavy-handedness of Anderson's earlier fiction. Missing here is narrative evasiveness, an overt undermining of meaning in language; instead, we are pretty much *told* things— especially concerning the social milieu of the times—as the author seems to believe himself. John O'Neill has recognized this disparity in "Godliness": "In language and form, . . . 'Godliness' is simpler, less innovative than most of the other stories in *Winesburg*." O'Neill may be a little too indulgent with the tale, however, when he goes on to praise it for contributing "to our sense of the scope and integrity of *Winesburg, Ohio* in its treatment of social and economic themes, and its fusion of sociological and psychological realities in the town."[10] Many other tales in the book do as much but in more evocative ways that necessitate the reader's participation in determining meaning. Nonetheless, Anderson does succeed in showing how religious tenets can both mold one's personality and be manipulated at the same time. A similar dynamic is at work in a more richly ironic way in "The Strength of God."

In "Tandy," the story that immediately precedes "The Strength of God," the narrator explains that the avowed agnostic Tom Hard was so intent on "destroying the ideas of God . . . that he never saw God manifesting himself" in his daughter (113). At the conclusion of "The Strength of God," Curtis Hartman reveals to a baffled George Willard that "God has manifested himself to me in the body of a woman," Kate Swift (124). It is tempting to surmise that the minister experiences a genuine epiphanic moment in this scene and indirectly confirms the narrator's comments from the previous tale that the presence of God can be found in another human being. However, to do so would require us to overlook much evidence in the story that suggests a contrary interpretation and would cajole us also into becoming as willfully deceived as the minister. For Curtis Hartman, like Jesse Bentley, consistently turns to his conventional religious upbringing as a way of justifying his behavior at any given moment. Ironically, although he often deviates from his religious tenets, he also feels compelled to turn to them to ferret out a validation for his actions. As in Foucault's Panopticism, Curtis constantly revaluates his actions in light of what he deems to be conventionalized religious precepts; he often

73

behaves as he wishes but only when he confirms that such behavior passes muster with presumably standardized and acceptable moral codes.

Curtis is so immersed in acceptable codes of behavior that we are never given access to any thoughts that might lie behind that safe behavior. As pastor of the Presbyterian Church, which "held itself somewhat aloof from the other churches of Winesburg," Curtis is a nonthreatening presence to his fairly smug congregation. Not a charismatic speaker, he endures "hardship" every time he has to preach to the congregation (117). "He was not one to arouse keen enthusiasm among the worshippers in his church but on the other hand he made no enemies" (117–18). His performance as pastor is validated by the banker's wife, Mrs. White, who throughout the book is the exemplum of staid convention. In addition, his "experience with women had been somewhat limited," and so he appears content with his wife, a model of respectability.

This unexciting but safe existence is tested when the minister first spies Kate Swift from the church bell tower, smoking in bed—an act that makes him "horror stricken." That a woman would be smoking—something that he has encountered only in the occasional novel—prompts him to deem her as "apparently far gone in secret sin" (118). Obviously titillated by this sight, Curtis must suddenly grapple with a "struggle [that] awoke" in him, for he desires to gaze upon her again, while at the same time convincing himself that *she* needs to be saved with the help of his sermons. Shocked out of his everyday complacency, he begins to inject some passion into his next sermon, which "attracted unusual attention because of its power and clearness" (118). Clearly, Curtis begins an unusual melding of growing sexual passion and pietistic zeal, because from this point on he interprets his every action connected with his blatant voyeurism as a test of faith. The narration follows his rationales closely all the while, though not without drawing attention to their apparent disingenuousness.

In an early instance, the minister methodically goes out for a walk, picks up a stone, and "rushe[s] off" to the bell tower to break a piece of a stained-glass window overlooking Kate's bedroom. When he sees her aunt, not Kate, raising the shade in the bedroom, the "minister almost wept with joy at this deliverance from the carnal desire to 'peep' and went back to his own house praising God" (120). The narrator points out, however, that "in an ill moment he forgot . . . to stop the hole in the window." Curtis views this scene as one in which he valiantly fought off temptation, but he fails to acknowledge to himself that *he* was the instrument of such temptation. He deviates from acceptable moral standards, but he couches such actions within the conventional codes of his faith. In another impromptu sermon to his congregation he para-doxically endorses his behavior by telling them that he had "surrendered to temptation" but was saved by the "hand of God"; accordingly, he turns his experience into a soothing balm for his parishioners: "As he [God] has raised me so also will he raise you. Do not despair" (120).

Still falling back on a knee-jerk conviction that God will intercede for him regardless of his actions, Curtis allows himself to proceed with his voyeurism at full speed. The narrator announces, "And now began the real struggle in the soul of the . . . minister" (121). "By chance," he finds out the time when Kate is in bed reading every night, and on the first night of his discovery he watches her for two hours. With deflated certainty, the narrator tells us that "he did not want to kiss the shoulders and the throat of Kate Swift and had not allowed his mind to dwell on such thoughts," even though soon after the minister admits to himself that his mind has indeed been "thinking of the shoulders and neck" of the teacher (122). The narrator provides some fore-casting of this later admission by stating in the next line, "He did not know what he wanted" (121).

After a moment of wavering faith, wherein Curtis blames God for his trial, he renews his rationalizations by vowing not to repair the broken window, rea-soning, "I will train myself to come here at night and sit in the presence of this woman without raising my eyes," behavior that will, he hopes, show him the "light of righteousness" (122). Removed of the pious justification, such a deci-sion merely gratifies his continued desire to peep at the teacher, peeping that continues from the fall into the winter, at which point he admits failing in his objective and finally resolves to "utterly give way to sin" and ultimately leave the ministry. In a momentary abandonment of his faith, he tells himself, "If my nature is such that I cannot resist sin, I shall give myself over to sin" (122). Now also hating his wife, he ends up sounding like the drunken stranger in "Tandy": "Man has a right to expect living passion and beauty in a woman" (123).

This temporary madness in Curtis is rather quickly extinguished, though, when he gazes at Kate presumably for the last time, seeing her naked, upset, and *perhaps* praying on her bed. This scene becomes the setting for an appar-ent epiphanic moment for the minister, for he rushes out of the bell tower and informs George Willard, "God has manifested himself to me in the body of a woman. . . . Although she may not be aware of it, she is an instrument of God, bearing the message of truth" (124). Proclaiming himself to be "deliv-ered," he unwittingly undercuts such a momentous scene by showing George his bleeding fist and attributing the "strength of God" as the agent behind his breaking the rest of the window, which now must be replaced.

In spite of the dramatic conclusion, Curtis's epiphany seems to ring hollow. First of all, throughout the tale he couches his prurient behavior in terms of his pious faith, and the tale concludes in this vein. Furthermore, the narration itself at the end is rather obscure in several key respects: the minister indeed seems to be startled when he believes Kate to be praying, for with "a cry he arose, dragging the heavy desk along the floor. The Bible fell, making a great clatter in the silence. When the light in the house next door went out he stumbled down the stairway and into the street" (124). In spite of such details, we never find out exactly when he broke the window—before or after the light in Kate's window went out? Surely the sound of breaking glass would have drawn her attention to the bell tower, as might Curtis's cry, the dragging of the desk, and the falling of the Bible. With the chronology of significant events purposely vague, we are left to wonder whether Kate Swift realizes that she has been the object of the minister's peeping. And in spite of his fevered condition, we may also wonder whether Curtis suspects as much—and if so, then his hysterical reaffirmation to George of his deliverance may be seen perhaps not as a genuine moment of realization but as a final (and permanent?) immersion into his conventional religious fervor. Rather than being a moment of clarity and insight, it may very well illustrate the minister's ultimate return to normalized morality. The final scene in the bell tower may signify his last act of delusion: it is only from his perspective that we are told that Kate is praying; perhaps she is simply sobbing after her encounter with George Willard. It is also from Curtis's point of view that the prostrate figure of the teacher resembles the figure of the boy with Christ in the stained-glass window, which is the very same window through which he has been gazing at her. So it really is not a stretch to hypothesize that Anderson not only presents us with a character who embraces his own moralistic delusion but also that the author cleverly spins his tale in such a way as to make it inviting for the reader to get swept away by it too.

After all, here is a person who has led an eminently safe life, with nearly every facet of that life regulated and on public display. It is little wonder, then, that when he is drawn out of his safe existence by passion—something difficult to neatly regulate—he tries to understand it by objectifying Kate Swift into a religious emblem and transforming his lustful voyeurism into a religious test. A further irony is that he may indeed have seen a manifestation of God in

Kate Swift during all of his viewings of her—the narrator tells us, for instance, that Curtis's sermons became impassioned and unscripted all this time and that he even became more affectionate toward his wife. However, the only way he can deal with his unregulated feelings is by sublimating them under his rigid orthodoxy, and as a result he remains a grotesque figure who reconfirms his static condition by the end of the tale. And in this story, unlike the "Godliness" tales just discussed, the narration successfully returns to a more evasive mode that invites us to accept the minister's interpretation of events while at the same time leaving us enough clues to suggest that what we are being told may not be essentially true.

As these several tales show, the influence of religion on these individuals who deem themselves godly men works in two ways. Their outlook on life is sharply formed by their religious beliefs, but they are not mindless, pious automatons who adhere to every tenet of their faith. Rather, they often manipulate their beliefs to accord with their own initiated actions. Thus the characters and their religious orthodoxy function as a series of checks and balances. However, as the conclusions of both "Terror" and "The Strength of God" illustrate, both men surrender their own will and finally subject themselves to the relative safety of their conventional beliefs, which serve as veritable life preservers for them but also as the final means of their self-delusions. Sexual or marital relationships also function in this dual manner in the book, and whereas Jesse Bentley and Curtis Hartman grapple with overt religiosity, a number of characters in other tales find themselves in a stymied conflict over society's sexual and marital codes.

. . .

As one of the earliest biographers of Anderson opined in 1927 and as countless other readers have stated since then, Anderson "seems greatly preoccupied with sex" in *Winesburg*.[11] Many of the stories already studied here focus on characters whose actions and thoughts are motivated, to some degree, by sexual passion or intimate relationships. But in these tales, other issues take center stage, with sexual topics serving as catalysts for these larger issues. In tales like "Paper Pills," "Mother" and "Death," "Adventure," "Surrender" (in tandem with parts of the second section of "Godliness"), and "The Untold Lie" issues like interpersonal intimacy and marital roles seem the primary focal point. In particular, most of the characters in these tales believe intimacy or marriage to be an essential (or *the* essential) means of achieving the understanding with another that would allow them to lead sentient, fulfilling lives. However, such characters either subject themselves or are subjected by others to shape their thoughts and actions according to static, formulaic conceptions of intimacy or marriage, with their actual experiences then failing to align with the static ideal; accordingly, such characters end up either frustrated or isolated and paradoxically further removed from achieving understanding with another.

But the subject gets even more complicated when it is situated within the larger societal context. For the characters in these tales, overt matters pertaining to sexuality are deemed aberrant or, at the very least, as topics that one assumes but does not openly discuss. As Foucault has observed, sexuality is a "domain susceptible to pathological processes, and hence one calling for therapeutic or normalizing interventions." Foucault also says that "power's hold on sex is maintained through language, or rather through the act of discourse that creates, from the very fact that it is articulated, a rule of law."[12] For these characters, who associate intimacy or sexuality with genuine fulfillment, understanding is forever out of reach, because their overt words or actions regarding sexuality are always gauged by this "rule of law," whether they themselves or others measure their behavior this way. When they succumb to these "normalized interventions," the result is usually failure and stagnation, and when they try to deny them altogether, the result is usually isolation.

By the end of "Paper Pills," we see Dr. Reefy resuming an isolated existence after the death of his wife. In the story's present, Reefy is a "forgotten old man," literally removed from any sense of community with anyone save his old friend, John Spaniard (18). He sits all day in his office, which seems hermetically sealed off by windows that he never opens. But in this forgotten figure, the narrator tells us, "were the seeds of something very fine" (18). Twice in this short tale the narrator compares the doctor to the "sweetness of the twisted apples," fruit that is rejected for sale to the cities because of its physical ugliness but that nevertheless is very delicious. But his future bride, "like one who has discovered the sweetness of the twisted apples," recognizes something special in the doctor, in spite of his physical unattractiveness (21). Perhaps part of the attraction is Reefy's conscious detachment from all social conventions and his apparent receptivity to behavior that diverges from such conventions. His unusual practice of making "paper pills" is directly related to this detachment.

Reefy makes it a habit to write down on scraps of paper "thoughts, ends of thoughts, beginnings of thoughts" from which he would form "a truth that arose gigantic in his mind. The truth clouded the world. It became terrible and then faded away and the little thoughts began again" (19). This passage clearly echoes the language of "The Book of the Grotesque," wherein individuals snatch up "a great many thoughts" and then themselves make the truths, which "were all beautiful" (9). In Reefy's case, though, the truths are "gigantic" and "terrible," suggesting that he may be aware of the danger of applying abstract truths to everyday life. Although he writes his thoughts down, he forms his truths in his mind, which implies that he is suspicious of the power of language to validate meaning. Instead, he allows his truths to "fade . . . away" and grinds his written-down thoughts into the hard paper balls that he later dumps onto the floor or throws at his friend. Like the old man in "The Book of the Grotesque" who never publishes his book, Reefy separates himself from the many thoughts and truths that he discovers. After furnishing us with these significant details about Reefy's character, the narrator then relates some significant details about the "tall dark girl" that eventually lead her to him.

Reefy's future wife—who interestingly goes unnamed throughout—comes to him after "a series of circumstances also curious" (20). For her, sexuality and marriage are intertwined not with fulfillment or happiness but with money. In the woman's story we see that the ideal of marriage, as is the case in several other tales, is evacuated of meaning because it is her rich inheritance that "set a train of suitors on her heels." Apparently also doubtful about the efficacy of language, the woman suspects that one suitor, who talked incessantly about virginity, was full of "a lust greater than in all the others" (20), and she ends up placing her trust in another suitor who "said nothing at all" but who gets her pregnant. Doubtful of idealized constructs and potentially a social outcast because of her pregnancy out of wedlock, she arrives at Reefy's office unknowingly receptive to another person of like mind. A key point here is that "without her saying anything he seemed to know what had happened to her" (20).

The two seem to achieve an intuitive understanding of each other—helped, in part, by the highly evocative scene she witnesses of Reefy's nonchalantly extracting a woman's tooth in his office. The pain and bloodshed produced by the extraction cause this woman and her husband to scream, but Reefy is nonplussed, while the "tall dark girl did not pay attention" (21). Lo and behold, the woman's pregnancy, we are told, "passed in an illness," very possibly in a way analogous to the tooth extraction. Reefy's knowledge of her problem without the need of an explanation, his apparent openness to her as a person undistracted by society's dictates about pregnant unmarried women, his

79

nonjudgmental "treatment" of her condition, and his seeming lack of interest in her inheritance suggest that the couple bond on a level that is unknown to society's regulated laws.

It is unusual, then, that she dies within a year of meeting Reefy, after they are married and after he starts reading "to her all of the odds and ends of thoughts he had scribbled on the bits of paper" (21). Perhaps Anderson chooses to have our understanding of their supposed harmony remain a mystery, as mysterious as the myriad thoughts that the doctor scribbles down. The larger point may be in the end result for Reefy: after his wife's death he leads a reclusive, isolated life, devoid of any connection to people except for his friend. He may still scribble his thoughts on scraps of paper and segregate himself from society's rules of conduct, but the picture we have of him in the present is hardly meant to be a viable alternative. Whereas the old man in "The Book of the Grotesque" wanted his bed propped up by his window to feel a part of the life outside, Reefy keeps his windows tightly shut and removes himself from interacting with others, his scribbled thoughts unexpressed to anyone else.

In "Mother," Elizabeth Willard is another character who doubts the efficacy of both language and society's codified constructs of sexual behavior but who struggles and fails to find any viable alternative. In her youth, we are told, Elizabeth was a restless free spirit, which accordingly earned her a "somewhat shaky reputation in Winesburg" (27). This restlessness was manifested by "an uneasy desire," both "for change, for some big definite movement to her life," and for a release through sexual passion (28). Both channels result in frustration for her, though: she pursues her desire for change through members of various theatrical companies who pass through the town, but they "did not seem to know what she meant." The results of her "second expression" were "always the same," in that her "strange wild emotions" went unrequited. Elizabeth's quandary is that in her early years she pinned her hopes for release and fulfillment onto abstract ideals that ultimately did not manifest themselves in practice. Consciously looking for "something unexpressed" in an understanding other always resulted in disappointment for her.

Elizabeth finds that her husband, Tom, is the embodiment of this disappointment, he being neither a source for "some big definite movement" nor a lover who satisfies her sexual passion. In fact, Tom seems to embrace the two sources of her defeat: the alluring power of language and society's nostrums. Elizabeth, who "listlessly" wanders through the dilapidated hotel "tall and gaunt," with "her face marked with smallpox scars," is an embarrassment to her "slender, graceful" husband, who deems his wife a figure "defeated and done for." Going about the town "spruce and businesslike," Tom fancies himself a potential big man in people's eyes. Elizabeth, however, like Anderson's other strong but defeated women, recognizes the duplicity of language and the false appeal of prescriptive codes; unable to find meaning and fulfillment any other way, though, she prays that her son George "be allowed to express something for us both" (23).

The narrator describes the relationship between mother and son as a silent one, although they share "a deep unexpressed bond of sympathy" (23). Hoping that George not become "smart and successful" in the conventional sense, Elizabeth recognizes that her son "is not a dull clod, all words and smartness. Within him there is a secret something that is striving to grow. It is the thing I let be killed in myself" (25–26). Elizabeth attempts to achieve her "girlhood dream" (23) through her son, viewing him as an extension of herself and projecting onto her husband the embodiment of every obstacle that "killed" the "secret something" in her.

It is clear that she regards her husband this way. The narrator tells us, "Although for years she had hated her husband, her hatred had always before been a quite impersonal thing. He had been merely a part of something else that she hated. Now, and by the few words at the door, he had become the thing personified" (27). So, when she feels that her husband may prevail in swaying George to think and act like him—to become a success and not act like a "gawky girl"—she experiences a "definite determination" to take action: to kill her husband and thus remove for her son the embodiment of society's obstacles.

But even though she views George as a partial extension of her unfulfilled hopes, Elizabeth herself apparently tries to force a "big definite movement" to occur, and with dramatic flourish, when she decides to adorn herself in costume before approaching her husband to murder him. Interestingly, the effect she strives for is to appear to her husband as someone else, "something quite unexpected and startling," a "figure" approaching its victim by stealth (29). The attempt is doomed for failure, however: besides the fact that her physical strength wavers, Elizabeth becomes an agent without an identity, vacillating between living through George and acting as a mysterious, dramatic performer. As in her youth, she still tries to force an epiphanic moment to occur, but the intensity of the moment is radically deflated when George quite innocuously tells her that he has rejected all of his father's advice. George does not think she understands, and she, wanting to "cry out with joy because of the words

81

that had come from the lips of her son," is unable to make him understand. Obviously relieved that her son intends not to embrace his father's ways, Elizabeth nonetheless remains in a stagnant condition. Incapable of exerting a "desire for change" herself, she at best experiences something close to it only through her son. In "Death," however, she becomes her own unwitting agent and achieves the momentary release that she had so long desired, and she does so through a nonverbal "divine accident."

Beginning several years before the story's present, "Death" depicts both Elizabeth and Dr. Reefy as individuals in search of "the same release," which they find unconsciously in each other in a moment of passion. Elizabeth visits Reefy's office ostensibly for her physical health but really for an understanding other to talk to. The narrator emphasizes how different they are physically, although "something inside them meant the same thing" (182). In the seclusion of the doctor's office, which is surrounded by the material refuse of a dry goods store downstairs, the two create a safe haven from external constraints in which they may freely communicate. The narrator emphasizes how the concrete reality of this setting and the very words they utter to each other are subordinated to the nonverbal emotions they elicit. Occasionally the doctor would make "philosophic epigrams," and then chuckle, we are told, and after periods of silence "a word was said or a hint given that strangely illuminated the life of the speaker" (183). The two seem to intuit that verbal communication can function as a catalyst for their desired "release," though their understanding on this point is not exactly in accord.

In a flashback, we learn that the eighteen-year-old Elizabeth yearned for a "real lover," someone who would help her find "some hidden wonder in life." Through all the "babble of words" of her several lovers, she endeavored to find the "true word" (184). In her recollections with Reefy, she associates a line spoken by one of her lovers, "You dear! You dear! You lovely dear!" as evoking "something she would have liked to have achieved in life" (183). The expression is inexact and richly suggestive, begging a precise meaning. In its original context—a moment of sexual passion—it certainly denoted both an emotional and a physical release. But as Elizabeth relates it to Reefy, it seems to transcend a purely sexual experience, defying a transparent, unambiguous meaning.

This way of using language seems to contrast with Reefy's way. As is shown in "Paper Pills" as well as in this tale, Reefy is fascinated with writing down thoughts and then formulating truths in his mind. Whereas a few fragments of a past sexual experience nebulously translate into something meaningful for Elizabeth, for Reefy precise epigrammatic statements are meant to carry much more significance, simply because they are uttered so definitively: "Love is like a wind stirring the grass beneath trees on a black night. . . . You must not try to make love definite. It is the divine accident of life" (183). The obvious irony here is that Reefy fails to follow his own sage counsel, and he affixes love to an abstract truth in the form of his pat definition. As his later actions with Elizabeth also demonstrate, he relegates love primarily to sexual passion, a presupposition that his patient unconsciously is striving to transcend.

In her youth, around the time she married Tom Willard, Elizabeth had resigned herself to believe that the very institution of marriage would "be full of some hidden significance" (185). She accepts society's opaque conception of marriage as representing the fulfillment of her desire for passion and "some big definite movement to her life," as the narrator puts it in "Mother" (28). She also turns to marriage as an antidote because her previous unmarried sexual experiences had earned her a tainted reputation in town. As she relates it to Reefy: "It wasn't Tom I wanted, it was marriage. . . . I didn't want to be a bad woman. The town was full of stories about me. I even began to be afraid Tom would change his mind" (186). Soon after she marries Tom, of course, she realizes that following the societal conventions of marriage provided no such release and, in fact, that it became a formalized instrument of stifling her. At the time, these pent-up feelings could find a temporary release only when she raced her horse out of town at breakneck speed: "I wanted to get out of town, out of my clothes, out of my marriage, out of my body, out of everything. . . . I wanted to run away from everything but I wanted to run towards something too" (187). Elizabeth wanted to extricate herself from every physical prop or token that reminded her of her staid condition, including the powerful and duplicitous effects of language (she yearns for the "true word"). Unable to find any concrete alternatives, though, she evolved over time into a physical and psychological grotesque, someone who would continually return in her mind to that period in her life when she might have found a more viable outlet than the static conventions of marriage. In "Mother" she nearly succeeds in transmitting her desire for a big change to her son; in "Death" she achieves a fleeting moment of "release," not through sexual passion but by transcending sexual passion.

As she becomes impassioned in retelling to Reefy her experience riding the horse, the doctor suddenly begins kissing her "passionately"; all the while, Elizabeth tries to continue with her story. The narrator's point of view in this scene is Reefy's, and so we are denied any insight into Elizabeth's mind. But

83

Reefy's reaction clearly demonstrates a moment of insight of his own. He utters the same evocative line as the earlier lover ("You dear! You lovely dear!") and "thought he held in his arms, not a tired-out woman of forty-one but a lovely and innocent girl who had been able by some miracle to project herself out of the husk of the body of the tired-out old woman" (187). Uncertain of Elizabeth's state of mind, we can be reasonably certain of Reefy's—that for a brief moment before they are distracted by men from downstairs throwing away garbage outside his door, he achieves something of the "divine accident" he had earlier spoken of: he recognizes Elizabeth's innate beauty in a moment of emotional release.

We might hypothesize, though, that Elizabeth does not share the experience, for all during Reefy's "love-making" she seems intent on continuing with her story. Perhaps that is why after this moment she begins "hungering" for death, a hunger that continues for nearly four years until George turns eighteen. In her final illness, "unable to speak or move and only with her mind and her eyes alive," she seems to spark a similar reaction of being moved from others, for "in her eyes there was an appeal so touching that all who saw it kept the memory of the dying woman in their minds for years" (189). Without words or physical passion—in other words, without the props she had long assumed were necessary—Elizabeth elicits understanding from others intuitively, with her eyes. But it is only in her death that she evokes understanding from her son.

We are told that on the day of his mother's death, George is "a little annoyed" because he was to have met Helen White later that evening for a date. Caught up with "his own affairs," particularly of what might have been with Helen, George is preoccupied with his own sexual feelings when he enters his mother's room to gaze on her body covered by the bed linens. It is at this moment, with his mind preoccupied with sexual thoughts, that George, unlike Reefy, distinguishes between sexual passion and recognizing and accepting the innate beauty of a person:

> George Willard became possessed of a madness to lift the sheet from the body of his mother and look at her face. . . . He became convinced that not his mother but some one else lay in the bed before him. . . . The body under the sheets was long and in death looked young and graceful. To the boy, held by some strange fancy, it was unspeakably lovely. (190)

He leaves the room in tears, and then acknowledges to himself, "My mother is dead." But then he states, "The dear, the dear, oh the lovely dear," a statement that is "urged by some impulse outside himself" (191). In death, the second expression of Elizabeth's "restlessness," her "uneasy desire" for a passionate release as alluded to in "Mother," becomes fulfilled through George. This is not an instance of obvious Oedipal fantasies being fulfilled, though. George utters a variation of the lover's line that negates the sexual intensity and underscores a love and understanding that is without any confines. First, his utterance is not made directly to his mother (he says "the dear" rather than "you dear"), and second, it is spoken without the passionate intensity by which it was rendered twice previously (as seen by the absence of exclamation points). This is not to say that Anderson rejects the uninhibited release of sexual passion; after all, the narrator concludes the tale by reminding us of the release that came to Elizabeth "but twice in her life, in the moments when her lovers Death and Doctor Reefy held her in their arms" (191). The spontaneity of sexual passion, its immediacy, does indeed provide a release from the web of society's codes and constraints. But it also lends itself to self-scrutiny by the participants as well as possible surveillance by others. Remember, for instance, how the minister, Curtis Hartman, becomes obsessed with rationalizing his passions for Kate Swift as a test of faith; and Elizabeth and Reefy, even in their moment of passion, allow that moment to pass when they hear others outside the door.

The epiphanic moment George experiences, however, is free of any need for scrutiny or surveillance. It serves as a crystallization of the fleeting moment between Elizabeth and Reefy, and it is perhaps illustrative of the "release" Elizabeth experiences with her other "lover," Death. Such an experience is indeed rare in the *Winesburg* tales, for even the tales that focus closely on sexual passion or the supposedly emotionally charged relationships of marriage show how such potentially liberating expressions often become instruments of frustration and failure when filtered through language and society's moral codes. "Mother" and "Death" are highly complex and wide-ranging portraits in which these issues converge; some of the other tales provide more focused and yet varied perspectives.

Several key events in "Adventure," for instance, are somewhat analogous to the scenes in "Death" in which Elizabeth both details why she finally submitted herself to marriage and describes her subsequent attempt to break out in her unbridled carriage ride. At sixteen Alice Hindman entered into a passionate

85

relationship with Ned Currie that compelled her to mold her future life around it. In the midst of their relationship, Alice, "betrayed by her desire to have something beautiful come into her rather narrow life" (85), allowed herself to be swept away by Currie's disingenuous words and the intensity of their relationship. "The outer crust of her life, all her natural diffidence and reserve, was torn away and she gave herself over to emotions of love." The narrator's choice of words is telling here: Alice found a release from the stolid confines of her surroundings not through any deep-seated love with Currie but through the "*emotions* of love"—a signal that she was swept away more by impulsive sexual excitement than anything else. This did have the effect, however, of emboldening her to defy the social codes that regulate proper relationships, because before Currie departed for a newspaper career in Cleveland, Alice had no qualms in offering to go with him as his unmarried partner: "Don't marry me now. We will get along without that and we can be together. Even though we live in the same house no one will say anything. In the city we will be unknown and people will pay no attention to us" (85–86). In spite of her liberated attitude, though, Alice succumbed to Currie's reassurance that he would return for her; in addition, she soon set the course of her future actions based on their impromptu sexual intercourse the night before Currie left town. From this act Alice resolved to herself that Currie would be forever hers, which suggests that she was still strongly influenced by conventional attitudes concerning sexual relations.

Sally Adair Rigsbee is partly correct in her comments on how women in *Winesburg* like Alice are shaped by society's codes of conduct: "Conventional sexual morality does nothing to protect women but actually contributes to their destruction. Alice Hindman's strength of character is undermined when her lover uses social conventions as a rationale for abandoning her and when she succumbs to the pressure to regard her spontaneous expression of love as binding."[13] But if Alice had the resolve to defy "conventional sexual morality" by insisting that she accompany Currie to the city unmarried, she hardly "succumbs to the pressure" of elevating Currie to the status of true lover because of their sexual intimacy. Instead, she *chooses* to fixate on Currie: "To her the thought of giving to another what she still felt could belong only to Ned seemed monstrous" (87). Alice succumbs to her own romanticized concept of finding a "real lover," as Elizabeth Willard had searched for in her youth. Regardless of the reasons, though, Alice evolves into an obsessive, lonely individual.

The duplicity of language is evident throughout the tale. Even as the years pass and with them the "beauty and freshness of youth," Currie's "words echoed and re-echoed through the mind of the maturing woman" (88). Her idealized vision of having a real lover also contributes to her growing isolation, for she is so entrenched in her rigid pattern of behavior that she seems unmindful of any other viable alternatives in her life. Although she eventually realizes that Currie is never going to return, she nonetheless demands "some definite answer from life" (90), still wishing for a concrete solution to her static condition. Asking herself, "Why doesn't something happen? Why am I left here alone?" (91) only reveals her continued reliance on the power of language to offer up from somewhere a simple, almost desperate corrective.

Alice finds a momentary corrective herself, an "adventure" that is spontaneous and devoid of a fixed meaning. As the narrator describes it in several ways, it is something outside of her static purview, a fleeting release akin to Elizabeth's heated carriage ride. We are told, for instance, that a "passionate restlessness took possession of Alice," a "strange desire took possession of her," a "mad desire to run naked through the streets took possession of her," and a "wild, desperate mood took possession of her" (90, 91). So confined is she in practicing the "devices of lonely people" that it takes some unidentifiable urging from outside herself to cause this sudden release, which effectively, though temporarily, serves a purgative effect for her. Shorn of the literal props of her society, feeling the "cold rain on her body," she achieves a brief instance of being free of society's proper codes and her own ascetic regimen. Not caring about the "possible result of her madness," she dares to confront the first person she meets. But when the old deaf man asks her, "What? What say?" she immediately drops "to the ground and lay trembling . . . frightened at the thought of what she had done" (91). The old man's innocuous questions create an instantaneous linguistic frame around her experience that anticipates a rational explanation, which she cannot provide. Pinned down by the precise questions, Alice is again self-conscious about her actions and resumes her former role, ultimately "trying to force herself to face bravely the fact that many people must live and die alone, even in Winesburg" (92). Alice realizes that the anonymity she had wished for in the city with Currie ("In the city we will be unknown and people will pay no attention to us") is not limited by geographical boundaries or population numbers. Her realization is also an indirect and unconscious admission that perhaps life in the city, where people "do not have time to grow old" (89), would have resembled life in Winesburg. To the reader, such a life is resigned to stratified gender roles and the elusiveness of language being firmly in place.

More in line with Rigsbee's assessment that the women in *Winesburg* succumb to outside pressures in their social and gender roles is the character Louise Hardy, from the second and third parts of "Godliness." It is telling that the narrator provides our first glimpse of Louise strictly from the point of view of the town, which is highly critical of this emotionally pent-up and reclusive figure. Her marriage to the respectable banker John Hardy was not a happy one, we are told, and "everyone agreed that she was to blame" (51). "Her life, lived as a half recluse, gave rise to all sorts of stories concerning her. It was said that she took drugs and that she hid herself away from people because she was often so under the influence of drink that her condition could not be concealed" (51). Mirroring Elizabeth Willard and Alice Hindman's attempts to break out of their static lifestyles, Louise would drive her horse and carriage "at top speed through the streets," never swerving to avoid pedestrians: "To the people of the town it seemed as though she wanted to run them down" (52). Further, the narrator informs us casually that she once set fire to her house and that she threatened her husband's life with a knife. From the town's conventional vantage point, Louise merits their disdain because she appears discontented both with her role as wife and mother and with her elevated station in the town. To explain such baffling behavior, the town views her as a drug addict and drinker, someone mentally unhinged for no other discernable reason.

We are provided a clue in the second part of "Godliness," though, that Louise is still capable of displaying deep-seated love and affection—for her son David, at least, whom she otherwise keeps at an emotional distance from her. On one occasion, David cannot bear to enter his parents' unhappy home and subsequently gets lost in the woods, only to return hours later after the town believes he was kidnapped. When he encounters his waiting mother, she overwhelms him with loving attention, which prompts him to think "she had suddenly become another woman," whose face "had become . . . the most peaceful and lovely thing he had ever seen" (53–54). Louise's chilling detachment reasserts itself, however, when her decidedly unloving father, Jesse, successfully bids to have David live with him on the farm; she resigns herself to her father and husband's wishes without a murmur of protest. The narrator provides other information that sheds insight into Louise's behavior: "The loss of her son made a sharp break in her life and she seemed less inclined to quarrel with her husband" (55). Such a resigned and defeated attitude is interpreted as peace and contentment by no less a figure than her husband, John, who "thought it had all turned out very well indeed." These momentary glimpses into the causes of Louise's frustrated life are expanded in the third part of the tale, "Surrender," in which the narrator intercedes for Louise in explaining some of the sources of her pent-up frustration; the narrator must step in because unlike most characters in the other tales, Louise does not have a viable opportunity to communicate freely to anyone.

As he did with Enoch Robinson throughout "Loneliness," Anderson's narrator interposes conjectures and explanations throughout "Surrender" that subtly imply that Louise Bentley is continually denied both a voice and a chance at unfettered contact with another. Also as in "Loneliness," in "Surrender" some of the conjectures function as red herrings that ultimately underscore the impossibility of the narrator's precisely explaining Louise's predicament.

The narrator begins with rather broad strokes, informing us too simply that Louise's is "a story of misunderstanding" and that "Louise was from childhood a neurotic, one of the race of over-sensitive women that in later days industrialism was to bring in such great numbers into the world" (62). Presenting Louise as a prototype of high-strung modern women seems rather a dodge, however, in light of the events detailed in the story. It is true that Louise deludes herself into thinking that a relocation from her father's farm to the Hardys' respectable household in town is a "great step in the direction of freedom," because she believes that in town "all must be gaiety and life" (63). It is also true that Louise seems to fulfill Albert Hardy's modern ideal that education is the key to advancing in life (he boasts to his daughters, for instance, "Everyone in Winesburg is telling me how smart she is" [64]). But, first of all, the contrast between farm and town lifestyles rings hollow, because both prove to be isolating experiences for Louise. In addition, Louise excels in school not out of any modern idea that she will rise up in the world but because "she was embarrassed and lonely" living with the Hardys.

What motivates Louise's actions from childhood on is her "wanting love more than anything else in the world and not getting it" (62). It is from this basic human emotion that Louise acts, and it is others' misunderstanding of her, shaped largely by their static conceptions of such societal functions as courtship and sexual intimacy, that helps mold Louise into a "neurotic." On the farm, without a mother and having a father "who did not look with favor upon her coming into the world," Louise turns to life in the town as a viable alternative for providing meaningful relationships. But denied the friendship of the Hardy daughters, she turns to their brother, John, not initially out of sexual desires ("it had as yet no conscious connection with sex") but only because "he was at hand" (66). Louise hopes that in John "might be found the quality she had all her life been seeking in people." An equitable relationship with another, not the playing out of a courtship ritual that designates young women as either "nice" or "not nice," is what Louise hopes to find in John. It is an intensely personal and private dynamic she wishes for, one in which he would "tell her of his thoughts and dreams" and then "listen while she told him her thoughts and dreams" (67). Such an exchange is problematic, though, because neither person is effective in verbal communication; Louise hopes, for example, to achieve her galvanizing dialogue with John at night, for in "the darkness it will be easier to say things."

But it is "in the darkness" of the Hardys' parlor instead where Louise attains a newfound "knowledge of men and women" by watching Mary Hardy, "without words," initiate a romantic tryst with a man. From this moment on, Louise unwittingly realigns her ideal with the more conventional trappings of adolescent courtship. She writes a note to John, trying "to be quite definite about what she wanted": "I want someone to love me and I want to love someone" (68). The fairly equitable relationship she had envisioned earlier mutates into the more traditional notion "that to be held tightly and kissed was the whole secret in life," as well as into the "age-old woman's desire to be possessed" (68). When John finally responds to her note, he does so having interpreted it in purely sexual terms: "That was not what she wanted but it was so the young man had interpreted her approach to him, and so anxious was she to achieve something else that she made no resistance" (69). The two rush into marriage when they mistakenly believe Louise to be pregnant, with John apparently already set in being incapable of understanding his new wife. During their first year of marriage, for instance, whenever she "tried to talk" of the more heartfelt reasons why she wrote that letter, John, " filled with his own notions of love between men and women, . . . did not listen but began to kiss her upon the lips" (70). Perhaps as a foreshadowing of Dr. Reefy's sudden, passionate kissing of Elizabeth in "Death," the scene ends up confusing Louise, who, the narrator feebly admits, "did not know what she wanted." Cut off from a loving relationship with her father, Louise remains without a loving relationship with her husband. Betrayed by the wordless—but still highly prescriptive and influential—societal codes dictating courtship and sexuality, Louise succumbs to a hasty marriage in part to avoid the label of being a "not nice" girl had she been really pregnant. Her inchoate but liberating ideal of an equitable partnership based on understanding has no place within the unyielding confines of the town. Louise becomes like one of Foucault's inmates who feel compelled to conform to normalized codes of behavior in order to gain acceptance. The respectable veneer of marriage is in this instance a more safely acceptable scenario than any such alternatives that would deviate from or challenge the expected norms. The narrator, too, who was so definite about Louise earlier in the tale, in the end abandons interposing any assertive explanation for her frustration, so that language's failure to be a clear means of communication is underscored. Marriage also becomes an act of abandonment for Louise—a formal negation of her desire to find substantive meaning in a relationship.

A similar conflict that emerges from society's construct of marriage is found in "The Untold Lie." Throughout this tale, the narrator juxtaposes images of natural beauty and liberation with the images of failure and confinement associated with marriage. Walter Rideout has called the story "a triumph of simplicity masking complexity," and indeed it seems at first glance to offer too neat a contrast that favors "private revolt against public convention."[14]

Ray Pearson, a "quiet, rather nervous man of perhaps fifty" (165), is a henpecked husband with six children, an overworked common laborer who lives in a "tumble-down frame house." As a young man, Ray's destiny became fixed after "something had happened" between him and his future wife; he sums up his life with the line, "Tricked by Gad, that's what I was, tricked by life and made a fool of" (167).

In contrast to Ray, Hal Winters is a young man, not, as the narrator emphasizes, from a respectable family in town of the same name but the son of Windpeter Winters, "who was looked upon by everyone in Winesburg as a confirmed old reprobate" (165). The narrator is meticulous in recording the town's damning judgment of the Winters clan: after Windpeter dies when he races his horses head-on into an oncoming train, "everyone in our town said that the old man would go straight to hell and that the community was better off without him"; about Hal the opinion was, he "was a bad one. Everyone said that" (166). Although only twenty-two, Hal "had already been in two or three of what were spoken of in Winesburg as 'women scrapes.'" He works on the same farm as Ray does only to be near a schoolteacher who is interested in him. "Everyone who heard of his infatuation for the school teacher was sure it

91

would turn out badly" (166). In the opening pages, then, the narrator sets up, perhaps too emphatically, the chief conflict of the tale: what Ray's sought-after advice will be to Hal, who has gotten the schoolteacher pregnant.

Both men share the belief that marriage is a prison resulting in a man's being "harnessed up and driven through life like a horse" (167). Hal antici-pates what Ray *should* advise him to do: "I know what every one would say is the right thing to do, but what do you say? Shall I marry and settle down? Shall I put myself into the harness to be worn out like an old horse?" And Ray, cognizant of the "proper" course of action Hal should take, "knew there was only one thing to say to Hal Winters, . . . only one thing that all his own train-ing and all the beliefs of the people he knew would approve, but for his life he couldn't say what he knew he should say" (168). As in the situation Louise Bentley and John Hardy found themselves in, the two men here regard mar-riage not as a freely chosen bond of love and understanding but as a solution that is chosen for people; premarital sex is a societal taboo, but "everyone" tacitly consents to marriage being the *only* course of action when such inter-course takes place.

The setting for Hal's confrontation with Ray causes Ray to avoid the pat response that "all his training" dictates. The beautiful autumn landscape awak-ens a "spirit of protest" in him; the unbounded beauty and expanse of nature allow both men apparently to feel emancipated from the rigid expectations of the town so that "from being just two indifferent workmen they had become all alive to each other" (168). Not only are their concerns about society's tenets suddenly insignificant, but even their delegated social roles as common la-borers ("indifferent workman") are momentarily devoid of meaning. The two men are free of all social codes of behavior and the judging eyes of the town. The narrator is consciously imprecise in articulating the effect the moment has for Ray: "The beauty of the country about Winesburg was too much for Ray on that fall evening. That is all there was to it" (169). This fleeting epiphanic moment for Ray returns when he seeks out Hal later that evening to finally give him his advice. Running across a field, "he shouted a protest against his life, against all life, against everything that makes life ugly" (169). But this moment is even more fleeting than his earlier one with Hal, for Ray essen-tially confuses liberation with a childlike sense of irresponsibility.

Running across the field, eager to tell Hal not to marry the teacher, Ray's thoughts focus on both puerile images of liberation and an equally juvenile evasion of personal responsibility. He recalls "how at the time he married he had planned to go west . . . how he hadn't wanted to be a farm hand, but had thought when he got out west he would go to sea and be a sailor or get a job on a ranch and ride a horse into western towns, shouting and laughing and waking the people in the houses with his wild cries" (170). As an adult he supplants these romanticized dreams of youth with his opinion that he has been "harnessed" into marriage because of children: "They are the accidents of life. . . . They are not mine. . . . I had nothing to do with them" (170). Perhaps the beauty of the landscape "was too much for Ray," for he associates his sudden feeling of emancipation only with images of complete abandonment, unbridled by both society's codes and any semblance of personal, inner moral codes.

In contrast to Ray's abandonment of all moral codes, Hal's final decision provides the story's highly nuanced sense of irony, for he initiates a kind of "private revolt against public convention" by *choosing* to marry the schoolteacher. As he tells Ray, "Nell ain't no fool. . . . She *didn't ask me* to marry her. I *want* to marry her. I *want* to settle down and have kids" (170, emphasis mine). Unlike Louise and John—unlike, too, Ray and his wife, who get married because they feel compelled to—Hal makes the decision his own, and thus takes on the responsibility himself. He does not submit himself to society's prescribed formula or to Ray's brief fascination with utter abandonment but becomes instead an independent actor. Thus the narrator's earlier contrast of the radical deviance of the Winters clan with Ray's defeated submission to marriage ends ironically by the tale's conclusion; the irony, however, lies in Hal's radical decision to *want to* get married, for reasons that defy society's scripted expectations, which deny personal choice and dictate the choice to be made.

The tales in this grouping demonstrate the usually conflicting and often contradictory relationship between the individual and society toward sexual intimacy and marriage. In some instances, such as those involving Elizabeth Willard in "Mother," Alice Hindman in "Adventure," and Dr. Reefy in "Death," the psychological release provided by sex becomes confused with mere physical gratification. In other instances, the hope of gaining a loving, understanding relationship with another is betrayed by the influence of prescribed notions of gender roles, which individuals often either blindly submit to or consciously manipulate. The stifling effects of prescribed gender roles are apparent in the desperate actions that Elizabeth, Alice, and Louise Bentley choose to take. The public token of a loving, understanding relationship, marriage is portrayed sometimes as a superficial panacea to life's ills and sometimes as an enforced sentence for taboo sexual behavior. And hanging over all of these characters' actions that involve sex is the atmosphere of surveillance, because, though sex is an integral component of life, a conscious attention to the subject is nonetheless always held suspect by various sources in society and even by the individual. For many of these reasons, really none of these characters achieves a fruitful or sustained release from their frustrated lives. The "thing needed" (200) that would allow them to emerge from the condition of the modern grotesque remains elusive for them. But Anderson shows us that such a "thing," as inexpressible as it may be, can be gotten; he shows us this in George Willard.

. . .

George Willard appears in most of the *Winesburg* tales and is the center of attention in several of them. As mentioned earlier, however, because he is not a consistent presence in the book and is a passive one in most of the tales, it is the most speculative of interpretations to read the book as a *bildungsroman,* and it is just as speculative to view George as the old writer in "The Book of the Grotesque," even "symbolically if not actually."[15] But because George plays a significant role in a number of tales, specifically "Nobody Knows," "The Teacher," "An Awakening," "Sophistication," and "Departure," Anderson does allow us to discern at least the rudiments of a pattern of growth in him.[16] It is impossible to ignore such a pattern; however, because Anderson is not writing a traditional novel with a clearly identified protagonist and plot line, opting instead for fleeting glimpses into the lives of many individuals, we must also consider the depiction of this character in each individual tale. And to do so would suggest that for most of the book—very nearly all of it—George seems to confirm Seth Richmond's negative opinion that "George belongs to this town" (107). George may indeed "belong" to Winesburg but only insofar that he shows himself prone to embracing the wide array of truths that the other characters featured in the book fall victim to.

In the tales in which George features prominently, we can see him succumbing to various sources of power in society that dictate prescribed codes of behavior; again in a Foucauldian sense, we can also see him be the willing agent of his own subjection to these truths. In addition, we can find numerous instances in which George is fascinated with language: how it induces prescribed action and how it provides a semblance of objective meaning and, eventually, how it can be manipulative and how it is ultimately an unreliable means of achieving genuine understanding. On this level, George's experiences in these several tales do serve as a microcosm of the varied experiences of the characters detailed in the other tales. He shows himself to be subject to the expectations of the town, particularly concerning sex and gender roles; he willingly submits himself to popular myths, such as that of the writer's life; and he implicates himself in reaffirming class distinctions. But besides his frequent appearances throughout the book, what distinguishes George from the other victims of the modern grotesque is that he discovers a viable, non-verbal means of communication; this leads to an intuitive understanding that is the antidote to the modern grotesque. In the penultimate tale, "Sophistication," Anderson allows George to discover the "thing needed" that "makes the mature life of men and women in the modern world possible" (200).

But in the first tale in which George plays a major role, "Nobody Knows," he is greatly inhibited from making such a discovery. Induced into an "adventure" by an inviting note from Louise Trunnion, George apparently has his first sexual experience. Rather than it being a liberating experience, as so many other characters also mistakenly believe sex to be, George's sexual encounter underscores how immersed he is in societal expectations regarding sex, gender roles, and class division. Moreover, George fully succumbs to the language that articulates such expectations.

George shows himself to be a naif concerning matters of sex both at the very beginning and at the end of the tale. His relative innocence about entering into a brief affair makes him feel that he is under surveillance, for he proceeds to Louise's house by stealth. On leaving the newspaper office, he looks "cautiously about" and exits "hurriedly"; he walks on "carefully and cautiously," purposely "avoiding the people who passed" (38). Like Wash Williams and his inexperience with women, George thinks it would be an "exquisite pleasure" simply to touch the folds of Louise's dress. After his experience, while walking home, his newfound confidence is shattered when, in the darkness, he stops cold, "attentive, listening as though for a voice calling his name" (41). He can only regain his confidence by reverting to the cocky, masculine attitude he assumed when he met Louise earlier: "She hasn't got anything on me. Nobody knows" (41). George can be assured of this only because he has embraced conventional notions about masculinity while seeming fully aware of Louise's tainted reputation in town.

The narrator subtly paints a rather squalid picture of Louise's life: when George spots her in her house, she is working in a "little shed-like kitchen"; the neighborhood is a hodgepodge of houses and miniscule attempts at farming (a "narrow potato patch" fills the front lawn of the house, and elsewhere in the neighborhood are vacant lots between homes where corn grows); Louise's face is smudged with dirt; and her gingham dress is soiled. Living financially on society's margins, Louise is also morally outside the pale, a fact that interestingly goads George into becoming a man by conventional standards. As the narrator explains, "Doubt left him. The whispered tales concerning her that had gone about town gave him confidence. He became wholly the male, bold and aggressive. In his heart there was no sympathy for her" (40).

Their encounter becomes a self-fulfilling prophecy goaded on by the alluring power of language. Town gossip deems Louise to be a tramp, and so George acts accordingly, using a "flood of words" as his means of asserting his superiority. Afterward, George presumably tells all to a drugstore clerk from whom he buys a celebratory cigar: "George Willard felt satisfied. He had wanted more than anything else to talk to some man" (41). In effect, George becomes complicit in the town's efforts to pass judgment on such deviants as Louise. His newfound identity may suffer a temporary lapse at the end, but he regains it by reassuming the mantle of masculine and class superiority, as encoded in the town's prescriptive rhetoric. In this tale, George unquestionably accepts the rhetoric as the truth.

"The Teacher" is a complex tale in which both the meaninglessness of words and attempts at achieving nonverbal understanding clash in Kate Swift's relationship with George. Up until this point in the book George has advanced from being afraid of inquiring into people's lives—as evidenced by his comments after Wing Biddlebaum dismisses him in "Hands" (14)—to having a more probing, earnest interest in them—as shown by his insistence to Enoch Robinson that he continue with his story in "Loneliness" (143). At the same time, though, he displays a tendency to accept various prescriptive codes of behavior on a literal level, as his attitudes about gender roles in "Nobody Knows" and his romanticized notions of the writer's life in "The Thinker" illustrate. But in his former teacher, Kate Swift, George encounters someone who strives with a passionate intensity to jar him from such a tendency, to urge him to reject being a "mere peddler of words" (131). George misinterprets Kate's attempts, however, because both characters—but especially George—confuse passionate nonverbal understanding with sexual passion. Kate, like Elizabeth Willard and Louise Hardy, also succumbs to such confusion, but unlike Elizabeth and Louise she does so momentarily, dispelling the confusion by actually beating George with her fists. By the end of the tale, Kate may indeed have been an "instrument of God," but for George, not Curtis Hartman; alas for George, her message, like God's ways, remains mysterious.

Ostensibly "concerning Kate Swift," the tale begins and ends by focusing on George. At the beginning, which is set on the morning before their final encounter, George ruminates over a meeting he has just had with the teacher, who "had talked to him with great earnestness," but with the result that George "could not make out what she meant by her talk" (126). By the end of the story, he seems just as confused, although he is now dimly aware of a deeper meaning in their last meeting, as he speaks aloud to himself: "I have missed something. I have missed something Kate Swift was trying to tell me" (133–34). This last remark does not indicate a dramatic change in George, but it does suggest that he has gained a glimmer of insight that was lacking at the beginning of the tale.

After their earlier encounter, George had also spoken aloud to himself, but his spoken thoughts concerned only the prospects of a physical, sexual connection between them: "Oh, you're just letting on, you know you are. . . . I am going to find out about you. You just wait and see" (127). This thought, about finding out about Kate, occurs immediately after the narrator describes at length George's extensive efforts to put to bed the latest issue of the newspaper. Perhaps the narrator is hinting that George entertains the thought of digging up information about the teacher as the town's official reporter—an action that will be dismissed implicitly by Kate when she tells him not to be a peddler of words and that the "thing to learn is to know what people are thinking about, not what they say" (131). Furthermore, earlier in the tale, when George retires to bed, he does so hugging his pillow with "lustful thoughts" of Kate, thoughts that he then transfers to Helen White, "with whom he had been for a long time half in love" (127). At the end, he again hugs his pillow, but this time "he tried to understand what had happened" in his last encounter with Kate and with Curtis Hartman's surprise visit—"He could not make it out. Over and over he turned the matter in his mind" (133). In this tale George undergoes a subtle but clear transition. And it is Kate Swift, the "most eagerly passionate soul" in the town (130), who is the instrument of this change.

Appropriately, the thirty-year-old teacher is not of the town's—or the larger society's—mind-set. Having led an "adventurous" life traveling afar and leading a life that was "still adventurous" as a teacher, Kate is a strong-willed, independent woman. Accordingly, "There was something biting and forbidding in the character of Kate Swift. *Everybody felt it*" (129, emphasis mine). The

97

narrator neatly establishes a dichotomy between the staunchly conventional town and Kate: "The people of the town thought of her as a confirmed old maid and because she spoke sharply and went her own way thought her lacking in all the human feeling that did so much to make and mar their own lives" (130). But whereas she succeeds in inspiring her pupils to imagine and dream, as her tales of Charles Lamb and Benvenuto Cellini illustrate, she achieves at best a muted success in her "passionate desire to have [George] understand the import of life" (131) because she momentarily confuses that "passionate desire" to inspire with sexual passion. And George, who still regards himself as playing a traditional masculine role, contributes to the confusion.

As the narrator relates it, in her final meeting with George, late on that snowy evening, "she talked with passionate earnestness. The impulse that had driven her out into the snow poured itself out into talk. She became inspired as she sometimes did in the presence of the children in school" (132). But in her zeal to make her promising former student understand, "her passion . . . became something physical." This kind of nonverbal insight between two people, which the narrator often describes in the passive voice, is on the verge of occurring but misfires: "As she looked at George Willard, the passionate desire to be loved by a man . . . took possession of her. In the lamplight George Willard looked no longer a boy, but a man ready to play the part of a man" (132). It is only her sudden act of striking George with her fists that disrupts the moment. It is telling, though, that on this occasion Kate resorts to nonverbal means to end the misunderstanding between George and her; on the previous night when they met and were on the verge of physical intimacy, Kate resorted to some off-the-cuff words ("What's the use? It will be ten years before you begin to understand what I mean" [132]) to dispel the misdirected moment. In abandoning words, Kate follows her earlier advice to George, in a scene reminiscent of one between Wing and George in "Hands": grasping his shoulders, she tells him to "stop fooling with words" (131). (Recall that Wing, in a similar moment, tells George, "From this time on you must shut your ears to the roaring of the voices" [14].) Although he is aware that his moment with Kate held some meaning beyond that merely of a sexual nature, George is as yet unable to intuit her intentions. But as Anderson will explore further in "Death" and "Sophistication," he here displays a rather postmodern distrust of language and hints that nonverbal communication may be the key to understanding and transcending grotesqueness.

Interestingly, it is again through nonverbal means—and again involving the striking of blows—in "An Awakening" that George shows further signs of achieving an intuitive understanding. For much of the tale the narrator sets up a series of contrasts in the thoughts and actions of Belle Carpenter, George Willard, and Ed Handby, contrasts that showcase public appearances and expectations; the eventual rendezvous involving all three serves to undermine such appearances and expectations, with the result that George again flirts with a moment of insight.

In the early pages we are given a double-edged portrait of Belle's life: on the surface, she is a member of a respectable family, the daughter of a bank bookkeeper, and because of this proper background, "She did not think that her station in life would permit her to be seen in the company of the bartender," Ed Handby (146). The reality of her existence is quite different, though. Belle despises her father, whose "life was made up of innumerable pettinesses" and who mistreated both his wife and daughter. Belle is so pent up with rage against her conditions that "when black thoughts visited her she grew angry and wished she were a man and could fight someone with her fists" (145).

By the town's standards, Ed Handby is definitely someone from a lesser "station in life" than Belle. A bartender of thirty who lives above the saloon he works in, Ed has the reputation in town for leading a dissolute life; for instance, when he squanders a sizable inheritance on "an orgy of dissipation," the "story . . . afterward filled his home town with awe" (146). But in spite of his brazen reputation, Ed is convinced that Belle "was the woman his nature demanded and that he must get her," whereupon he begins to save money "for the support of his wife" (147). Unable to verbally communicate, either honestly or even through conventional platitudes, it is "with his body he expressed himself" (147). No doubt it is this direct, forceful approach to dealing with life that Belle finds so alluring. As if to emphasize the potential physical force in Ed, the narrator repeatedly mentions his fists, while tempering such descriptions by pointing out that Ed's voice was soft, "as though striving to conceal the power back of the fists" (146).

George Willard, meanwhile, is first described lounging about the local poolroom, apparently unheedful of Kate Swift's advice that he "stop fooling with words" because he is so eager to make masculine boasts: "The pool room was filled with Winesburg boys and they talked of women. The young reporter got into that vein. He said that women should look out for themselves, that the fellow who went out with a girl was not responsible for what happened. As he talked he looked about, eager for attention" (147). George again succumbs to de rigueur beliefs regarding gender roles, particularly toward masculine power. Excited by the conversation, he wanders into a poor section of town muttering words, literally captivated by language as if it had the authority of a magic spell—"Hypnotized by his own words, the young man stumbled along the board sidewalk saying more words" (148). The words he utters initially entail law and order and discipline, and with such concepts in mind he finally takes in the shabby surroundings around him, which consist of cheap frame houses with animal pens in the back, and imposes a romanticized veneer on the squalid scene, based on his "reading of books . . . concerning life in old world towns of the middle ages" (149). Being entranced by the manipulative power of language, George feels "unutterably big and remade," "oddly detached and apart from all life" but nonetheless superior to such life. Now "full of big words" and imbued with a "sense of power" (151), he feels that he can exert such power over Belle effortlessly and overwhelm her into submitting to him. But the narrator cleverly shows how the power and illusion of language are essentially fragile and ineffectual when pitted against the nonverbal potential of force.

George's belief that language alone has such unequivocal, metamorphic powers is subtly undermined by the narrator, as when he tries to capture George's thoughts: "The desire to say words overcame him and he said words *without meaning,* rolling them over on his tongue and saying them because they were brave words, *full of meaning*" (150, emphasis mine). Furthermore, George seeks out Belle, thinking "she would understand his mood," but really he searches for her for sex, not understanding. When he finally meets her, he "talked boldly, swaggering along and swinging his arms about" (151). To George, his loquaciousness with Belle becomes a moment of domination: "The new force that had manifested itself in him had, he felt, been at work upon her and had led to her conquest" (152). Whereas Belle and Ed elude both conventional norms of behavior and the surveillance of the town (their affair "on the surface amounted to nothing" [147]), George up to this moment is immersed in both, as he was at the end of "Nobody Knows." He still appears as an unwitting agent of society's power forces.

It is only the nonverbal actions of Ed that startle George out of this mode of behavior. More violent than Kate Swift in her blows to George's face, Ed nevertheless "had power within himself to accomplish his purpose without using his fists" (153). The narrator emphasizes that the uncommunicative Ed refrains from using his full strength, in stating that Ed tosses George aside three times after he rises to confront him again, and that Ed "seemed prepared to keep the exercise going indefinitely but George Willard's head struck the root of a tree and he lay still." Ed does not behave like the unmannered wild man the town deems him to be. Belle does not behave like the helpless victim of George's "big words"; in fact, during their meeting, "she had not seemed to be listening to his words," waiting all along for Ed to appear. It is George, not Belle, who experiences "an awakening" in this tale. Perhaps the actions of Belle and Ed have a more jarring effect on him than those of Kate Swift, for when George returns home, he cannot bear to cross through the poor neighborhood again, "wanting to get quickly out of the neighborhood that *now* seemed to him utterly squalid and commonplace" (154, emphasis mine). He still may be baffled about what happened with Belle and Ed (as he was not certain what Kate was trying to tell him), but he has already discarded the romantic verbal constructs that he earlier used to distort the appearance of that poorer section of town. After the shock of reality replaces his idealized "conquest" of Belle, he is able to perceive the actual squalor of the neighborhood. He is able to "see" without the verbal props borrowed from books or the vaunted "big words" that hypnotized him. These reinforced traits will come to his aid when he finally "sees" the beauty of his mother in "Death" and when he discovers an alternate, nonverbal means of understanding in "Sophistication."

Between "An Awakening" and "Sophistication" we can see sporadic and yet more substantial glimpses of a maturing George Willard. In "'Queer'" and "Drink" George veers between a paranoid victim of self-surveillance (Ned Cowley in "'Queer'") and the relentlessly self-controlling personality (Tom Foster in "Drink"). George seeks out both characters and mostly succeeds in penetrating the public personas of each character without imposing his own judgment on them (although he does jealously resort to "protecting" Helen White's honor when Tom relates his fantasy of loving her). In "Death" George initially shows himself to be more absorbed with missing out on a date with Helen White than by the death of his mother. This is doubtless not meant to illustrate a reversal of character; Anderson throughout the book avoids presenting George as a novelistic, exemplary individual who matures in an undeviating fashion. Rather, George's absorption with Helen merely shows him to be human; at any rate, his preoccupation is only temporary, for he does make an intuitive connection with his mother when he recognizes her innate dignity and beauty and utters the words, "The dear, the dear, oh the lovely dear"

101

(191). This kind of understanding seemed beyond George's ability in "Mother." In that tale, after rejecting his father's formulaic advice for getting up in the world, he tried to make his mother understand but gave up. But it is only in "Sophistication" that we see George achieve an intuitive, nonverbal connection with an understanding other—and he and Helen are really the only characters in the book to do so. Throughout *Winesburg, Ohio*, Anderson presents numerous ways in which individuals become grotesques and attempt to find viable alternatives to their grotesqueness. As he could be only suggestive in diagnosing the modern grotesque in "The Book of the Grotesque," in "Sophistication" he is just as subtly evocative in prescribing a cure.

The narration of the tale is distinctive from the rest of the stories but is reminiscent in its telling of "The Book of the Grotesque," wherein the narrator seems close to explaining all for us but repeatedly draws attention to the fact that he can only approximate what the old man's intentions are and what grotesqueness means. In "Sophistication" the narrator comes even closer to explaining all—a tactic that Marcia Jacobson criticizes as being pompous[17]—except in the key concluding scene when George and Helen experience that unspoken moment of understanding. Up until this point the narrator intercedes not to tell all exactly but chiefly to illustrate the "sadness of sophistication" that George feels but is himself unable to express. For most of the tale the narrator and George are at cross purposes: while the narrator attempts to articulate the condition of sophistication and its impact on George and Helen, both characters struggle to avoid explaining it, either to themselves or to each other. And in spite of his elaborate and persistent attempts, neither can the narrator adequately articulate their *individualized* dilemma: he seems capable only of describing the dilemma in the abstract so that it approximates but does not precisely reflect George's and Helen's feelings and thoughts. At odds for most of the tale, the narrator's and George's intentions finally converge in the conclusion when the narrator resorts to a highly evocative approximation of what the moment means, saying only that each character got the "thing needed" from "their silent evening together" (200). "Sophistication" therefore demonstrates the victory of intuitive understanding over the constraints and imprecision of language, which throughout the book are shown to be instrumental in the process of individuals becoming grotesques.

Shortly after his mother's death and during the Winesburg County Fair, George meditates on feeling grown up and being ready to "leave Winesburg to go away to some city" to find newspaper work (192)—"Thoughts kept coming into his head and he did not want to think." Nevertheless he feels compelled to find "someone to understand the feeling that had taken possession of him after his mother's death" (193). Here, then, is the crux of the story—George is moved by feelings that he wants neither to think about concretely nor to articulate openly but that he nevertheless desires to share with an other: "With all his heart he wants to come close to some other human, touch someone with his hands, be touched by the hand of another. . . . He wants, most of all, understanding." The narrator, meanwhile, feels compelled to intercede for the reader in order to clarify George's inchoate feelings.

The narrator begins by trying to elevate George's feelings to an abstract, universal level: "There is a time in the life of every boy when he for the first time takes the backward view of life. Perhaps that is the moment when he crosses the line into manhood" (193). The narration continues in this abstract vein in describing the feelings of "every boy" and becomes uncannily similar to the description of how people develop into grotesques in "The Book of the Grotesque." It also closely echoes in wording Beaut McGregor's dream in *Marching Men:*

> Ghosts of old things creep into his consciousness: the voices outside of himself whisper a message concerning the limitations of life. From being quite sure of himself and his future he becomes not at all sure[,] . . . and for the first time he looks out upon the world, seeing, as though they marched in procession before him, the countless figures of men who before his time have come out of nothingness into the world, lived their lives and again disappeared into nothingness. The sadness of sophistication has come to the boy. With a little gasp he sees himself as merely a leaf blown by the wind through the streets of his village. He knows that in spite of all the stout talk of his fellows he must live and die in uncertainty. (193)

In trying to illustrate the "sadness of sophistication," the narrator hints that language itself is partly responsible for this condition because it easily lends itself to distorting reality. "In spite of all the stout talk" of others such as the Tom Willards, Jesse Bentleys, and Mrs. Whites, who embrace static but untenable formulas for living, one must accept the fact that the vicissitudes of life do not accord with such pat nostrums. In addition, as the story goes on to show, a distrust of prescriptive patterns of behavior will also prevent one from judging others according to how they measure up to such patterns. Throughout

103

the book grotesque characters are punished by various sources in society or even by themselves for deviating from normalized codes of behavior. Rejecting such codes allows one to recognize the innate dignity and beauty of others, no matter how repulsive or pathetic they *appear* to be. As the narrator explains, "One shudders at the thought of the meaninglessness of life while at the same instant, and if the people of the town are his people, one loves life so intensely that tears come into the eyes" (198).

In an earlier meeting, referred to twice in "Sophistication," George failed to achieve an understanding with Helen precisely because he was still caught up with the kind of "stout talk" that he displayed in "Nobody Knows," "The Thinker," and "An Awakening." In that previous meeting, he "had given way to an impulse to boast, to make himself appear big and significant in her eyes," "to say something impressive" to her (194, 195). Even though he realized that he was not adequately expressing his thoughts, he still persisted in relying on language to convey his mood: "In his desperation George boasted, 'I'm going to be a big man, the biggest that ever lived here in Winesburg'" (195). The narrator says that their time together then had "been rather stupidly spent," and George, "ashamed of the figure he had made of himself," recognizes that "now he wanted to see her for another purpose" (194).

Helen, too, has achieved a similar insight. As the narrator tells us, "she also had come to a period of change" (194). Spending time in the city while at college provides Helen with a different perspective on her life in Winesburg. In town with a pedantic instructor to attend the county fair, Helen at first shares her mother's superficial outlook, one that craves public notice and approval: "At the fair she was glad to be seen in his company as he was well dressed and a stranger. She knew that the fact of his presence would create an impression." But by the end of the day she grows "restless and distraught," in large part because of the vacuous chatter of the instructor and her mother. Originally from a small town, the instructor puts "on the airs of the city," and soon "his talk wearied the girl" (197), although it captivates her mother. Unable to tolerate the shallow banter any longer—"It seemed to her that the world was full of meaningless people saying words"—Helen flees in search of George, who at this moment is heading to the Whites' home. Both want to connect with the other, but neither will resort to using the kind of empty verbiage that George had earlier employed with her and that was on full display in the Whites' house. Their meeting this time will be marked by silence.

As they approach the fairground, the narrator again intervenes by attempting to provide an abstract framework to signify for us a *sense* of meaning in the scene. As Melville had provided a similar framework in the "Doubloon" chapter of *Moby-Dick* discussed earlier, the narrator here tries to establish, without setting down a definitive meaning for us, a context in which George and Helen experience their epiphanic moment. As the narrator explains, "In youth there are always two forces fighting in people. The warm unthinking little animal struggles against the thing that reflects and remembers" (198). The "older, the more sophisticated thing had possession of George Willard," and apparently it is this conscious mood that has George on the verge of becoming a grotesque himself, obsessing over the "sadness of sophistication." At the deserted fairground George and Helen do not sense the utter meaninglessness of life where, however, earlier that day "an American town worked terribly at the task of amusing itself" (192). Instead, the "sensation is one never to be forgotten. On all sides are ghosts, not of the dead, but of living people" (198). Still presenting the scenario in the abstract and probably mirroring but not precisely so the feelings of George and Helen, the narrator describes how in the midst of such apparent insignificance and meaninglessness one may "love life so intensely that tears come into the eyes." What helps George surmount the feeling of "his own insignificance in the scheme of things" is finding someone who can offer unequivocal understanding, without the need to talk and pass judgment and impose scripted solutions.

It is the mere "presence of Helen [that] renewed and refreshed him." Helen offers him no words of advice; her presence does not even rouse the prospect of a sexual release: "He wanted to love and be loved by her, but he did not want at the moment to be confused by her womanhood." They hold hands and they kiss, "but that impulse did not last" (199). Anticipating some kind of resolution to their dilemma, the narrator begins to abandon the abstract framework used earlier and resorts to more evocative intimations: "In that high place in the darkness the two oddly sensitive human atoms held each other tightly and waited. In the mind of each was the same thought. 'I have come to this lonely place and here is this other,' was the *substance* of the thing felt" (199, emphasis mine). In calling the pair "two oddly sensitive human atoms" who have sought out an "other," the narrator suggests that George and Helen connect without any social or gender or other linguistic referent; they achieve what David D. Anderson has called an "intuitive perception."[18] What they

105

"wait" for does not come by way of linguistic or any other concrete meaning, either. It evades articulated meaning.

On their return to town, the "spell that held them was broken," and they kiss again, but again they draw "quickly back from that impulse" (200). Now self-conscious of the moment they have just experienced, they revert to the "animalism of youth" "to relieve their embarrassment," and they "pull and haul at each other," laughing. As it was "the young thing inside him that saved the old man" from becoming a grotesque in "The Book of the Grotesque" (10), there is a similar intimation in this tale that a youthful outlook "chastened and purified" George and Helen, who play while running down a hill "like two splendid young things in a young world" (200). Having shared a deeply moving and yet fleeting experience, they do not allow themselves to be transfixed by it. As the old man chooses not to publish his insightful book and instead simply to continue engaging with and appreciating other people, George and Helen simply reenter everyday life "in dignified silence."

The narrator ends this climactic tale with an air of sweeping momentousness, but ironically he is quite determined that the object of the momentousness remain undefined, the reasons for its significance unknown, the actual maturity of the participants uncertain, and the staying power of the moment only temporary: "*For some reason* they *could not have explained* they had both got from their silent evening together the *thing needed.* Man *or* boy, woman *or* girl, they had *for a moment* taken hold of the thing that makes the mature life of men and women in the modern world possible" (200, emphasis mine). Avoiding the kinds of facile solutions that undermined his earlier works, Anderson in effect concludes *Winesburg, Ohio* with a resoundingly evasive but evocative solution. Language is too deceptive and unstable to contain it; any attempt to do so would ground it into an imitable formula that would make it susceptible to becoming either misunderstood, manipulated, or appropriated as another means of passing judgment on others. His "cure" for grotesqueness must be intuited, and such a cure is therefore boundlessly malleable and wholly contingent upon human subjectivity.

That "Sophistication" stands as the conclusion to "The Book of the Grotesque" underscores how disappointing "Departure" would be if it were the conclusion to a book that Anderson did not write—the story of George Willard. As Monika Fludernik has observed, "Indeed, [George's] departure from Winesburg is a let-down . . . and anti-climax."[19] Gauging it by conventional plot lines, the story is as baffling as it is frustrating. After achieving an intuitive understanding with Helen White, George delays his departure from town for a surprising five months; also, Anderson denies us a final scene between George and Helen, as she misses him on the train, and the importance of the occasion is undercut by the train conductor, Tom Little, who "had seen a thousand George Willards go out of their towns to the city" (203). Oddly following his father's warnings, George seems unduly preoccupied with not wanting to look like a "greenhorn." Only the last lines of the tale seem to accord with a traditional climax, detailing how, when George opens his eyes on the train, "the town of Winesburg had disappeared and his life there had become but a background on which to paint the dreams of his manhood" (204). Perhaps Anderson dashed off "Departure" hastily as a sketch, to round out George's story and conclude the book on a note of finality.[20] Perhaps it would be more compelling, though, to look at the tale as a self-consciously understated anticlimax instead, for doing so would further demonstrate how the book defies conventional expectations for fiction, while underscoring again how it displays postmodern sensibilities concerning language.

Throughout the sketch the narrator reminds us of the passing of time and how every solitary event is fleeting and mostly unremarkable to all but those most closely involved. As "Sophistication" showed, significant moments in individuals' lives do take place, but they do so without fanfare and they are devoid of plainly overt meaning. The "thing needed" for George and Helen remains interiorized, after all. In "Departure" the narrator illustrates the transitory nature of life by describing the seasonal changes in a landscape that George often sought out to "walk . . . in the silence" (202). The landscape remains essentially the same throughout the year, but with each season it presents a different appearance—a "smoky haze" hangs over it in summer, when men and machines harvest berries; the greenery of spring makes it look like a "wide green billiard table on which tiny human insects toil up and down"; in fall "bleak winds" blow down on it; and in winter it is covered with snow (201). Time is a continuum and does not stand still for any person or any event.

Many people in town wish George well on the day of his departure, but whereas the event has great significance for him, it is only of passing interest to the well-wishers. Some clerks on Main Street, for instance, ask, "Hey, you George. How does it feel to be going away?" On the station platform, "everyone shook the young man's hand," we are told, but these dozen or so people "waited about" for trains to take, not to see George depart. After their wellwishing, "then they talked of their own affairs." There are but two exceptions among all the townsfolk: Will Henderson makes a special effort to be out of bed to see him off, and a postal worker who "had never before paid any attention to George" seeks him out, tersely wishes him good luck, "and then turning went on her way." In such an atmosphere perhaps it is appropriate that Helen misses her chance "to have a parting word" with George. As "Sophistication" showed, words are not needed for people to achieve understanding. The person who uses the most words in the tale is George's father, who, as he did in "Mother," again resorts to conventional, clichéd advice that does little more than reaffirm one's subjection to society's surveillance: "Be a sharp one. . . . Keep your eyes on your money. Be awake. That's the ticket. Don't let any one think you're a greenhorn" (203).

Rather than emphasizing the momentousness of the occasion, the narrator instead hints at what may be of more lasting significance for George: "The young man, going out of his town to meet the adventure of life, began to think but he did not think of anything very big or dramatic. Things like his mother's death, his departure from Winesburg, the uncertainty of his future life in the city, the serious and larger aspects of his life did not come into his mind" (203). What George does think about are the myriad "little things" that he encountered on a daily basis in his casual interactions with others. No doubt his departure constitutes one such "little thing" for the many people who wish him well. In this commonplace setting we should perhaps not lend too much credence to Tom Little's thought that George is but one among thousands of young men who leave their small towns for the city or to the narrator's comment that "one looking at him would not have thought him particularly sharp" (203). From the town's superficial point of view, George's experience in setting out hardly causes a stir. Such a perspective, with its implied power to assess and judge, a power that has affected so many characters in the book—even George in several instances—now has little effect on him. He may momentarily submit to his father's concern that he "not . . . appear green," but when he settles in on the train, his memories of the "little things" take over, along with "his growing passion for dreams." It is these things— George's propensity to dream and his active memory—that have the potential not only to make him a writer but also to allow him to remain detached from society's dictates. It would be a mistake for the reader to attempt to assess whether the tale ends the book on a positive or a cautious note, for to do so would require one to interpret it in a conventional way common to popular novels. *Winesburg, Ohio* is far removed from plot-driven novels, and in "Departure" Anderson quietly presents us with an anticlimax of a provocative kind: in a nondescript manner, George Willard leaves Winesburg with little fanfare or applause from the town, but he is aware—as we are aware—that he has the proven potential to evade or surmount grotesqueness.

Having begun experimenting with innovations in using language and examining the modern grotesque in *Windy McPherson's Son,* Sherwood Anderson slowly advanced these themes in his subsequent novels *Marching Men* and *Talbot Whittingham.* All three are flawed works that nonetheless illustrate Anderson's gradual maturing both in his handling of these themes and in telling a story. *Winesburg, Ohio* is the culmination of his early experiments. By turning to short stories, he avoided the pitfalls of the plot-driven novel that had hampered his earlier works. But the short story also allowed him to harmonize form with content: his concern with the fragmentary nature of modern life is mirrored in the fragmentary glimpses he gives us of individuals in his short tales. Freed also from focusing on a dominant protagonist, Anderson is able to provide multiple perspectives on the modern grotesque. He provides glimpses into the lives of frustrated people who, imprisoned by language and the articulated codes of society, frequently resort to language—verbal expression—as a means of curing, or transcending, their grotesque condition, with the result that they remain grotesques. But in portraying characters who are, in effect, betrayed by the inefficacy of language, he cleverly employs a style of narration that draws attention to its own inadequacy in objectively telling the truth about their lives. And whereas in his early works he clumsily interjects pat solutions to the modern grotesque, in *Winesburg* he succeeds with his greatest innovation: what solutions there may be for the modern grotesque are to be found in fleeting moments of intuitive understanding that both reject language and rely on human subjectivity—on the part of both the individuals involved and the readers of the tales themselves. A foundational modernist work, *Winesburg, Ohio* is also a seminal precursor to postmodernism.

Epilogue

BEYOND THE GROTESQUES

When studied through the lens of postmodern theories of language and power, Sherwood Anderson's fiction yields rewarding new insights. This book, however, has been neither an exhaustive investigation of Anderson's works nor a study that examines them from multiple contemporary approaches. The intention is to establish new foundations in Anderson criticism upon which others might continue to build.

The question remains, which of Anderson's works would particularly benefit from such a fresh exploration? The purpose here is neither to take into account every book written by Anderson nor to provide a lengthy assessment of recent Anderson criticism. Some may argue with the selections presented here or the omissions. However, following Emerson's musings in "The American Scholar" on how books may be well used, the intention here is merely to inspire others to continue exploring Anderson from fresh perspectives.

There are critics who believe that Anderson's works, including those published after *Winesburg, Ohio,* merit a new exploration by scholars. David D. Anderson has observed that there "is a badly needed continued reassessment of [Anderson's] other works," particularly the novels that traditionally have been dismissed out of hand. David Stouck is one of the few critics within the last twenty years to reexamine such novels as *Many Marriages* (1923) and *Dark Laughter* (1925). In "Sherwood Anderson and the Postmodern Novel," Stouck breaks new ground in viewing these works as forerunners of post–World War II novels because of their consciously unreliable narration and fabulous content. James Scott Miller pursues a different but still rewarding look in a 1998 dissertation, examining *Dark Laughter* in terms of how Anderson and some of his contemporaries create a masquerade of racial identity in establishing the parameters of mainstream American culture.[1]

Other later novels such as *Beyond Desire* (1932) and *Kit Brandon* (1936) await interpretations from New Historicist or neo-Marxist or feminist perspectives. The former depicts Anderson's continued interest in the wide-ranging effects of industrialism, in this case, as they play out among the working class in Southern mill towns. The latter is an episodic tale following a young Southern woman as she runs away from home, spends time working in mills and factories, and eventually assumes a life of driving for bootleggers. By 1930 Anderson had begun traveling with Eleanor Copenhaver, a social worker with the YWCA who would later become his wife, throughout the middle Southern states, attending to male and female workers in predominantly textile mills.[2] In this milieu, in the midst of the Depression and during the growing national interest in socialism, Anderson had renewed his interest in the plight of working Americans, and in both works he grapples with the effects of a progressively mechanized nation on individuals and on larger communities; in particular he details working conditions in the mills, fragmentation in interpersonal relationships (reminiscent of earlier treatments in some of the *Winesburg* tales), labor strikes, and the ambiguous effects that organized socialism had on such communities. There has been no substantial critical treatment on either work that utilizes contemporary theories. Philip Greasley, though, has initiated an examination of *Kit Brandon* that studies how its narrative structure and linguistic forms emerge from oral storytelling traditions, which are "normally non-linear, episodic, or rambling"; Greasley thus intimates how postmodern theories of language might be employed fruitfully in regarding the novel. David Anderson, too, suggests that the characters and many incidents in *Beyond Desire* might be studied in terms similar to those applied to the grotesques in *Winesburg* or *Poor White*.[3]

Poor White (1920), the novel that most critics consider Anderson's best sustained effort, would indeed benefit from the kind of reading undertaken here of his early fiction, especially as to how Anderson continues his exploration of the modern grotesque. In Hugh McVey we have a man who molds his life around both the advice of his surrogate mother, Sarah Shepard—to be constantly active and achieving—and his fear of remaining poor white trash, like his father. Severely limited in communicating with language, Hugh finds expression and attempts to bond with others through his several laborsaving inventions. Not only do the characters Hugh and Clara Butterworth provide fine illustrations of individuals who strive to transcend the grotesque, but there are also numerous other characters—ranging from the rapacious Steve Hunter to Joe Wainsworth, the blacksmith who is destroyed by Bidwell's transformation—who furnish sharp portraits of industrialism's effects on individuals. The very transformation of the town—including the change in people's behaviors, the town's physical alteration, the influx of immigrants, and labor disputes—lends itself to New Historicist, neo-Marxist, and ideological interpretations. Oddly, there has been little recent criticism on *Poor White*, which perhaps of all of Anderson's novels deserves the most attention.

Many of the tales in Anderson's other short-story collections—*The Triumph of the Egg* (1921), *Horses and Men* (1923), and *Death in the Woods and Other Stories* (1933)—await contemporary theoretical interpretations. As David Anderson has argued, although the first two works are not as clearly cohesive as the *Winesburg* tales, each lends itself to being read, like *Winesburg*, as a short-story cycle. The opening sketch of *Triumph of the Egg*, "The Dumb Man," sets a tone for the rest of the book as much as "The Book of the Grotesque" does for *Winesburg*. In particular, Anderson revisits in this work and throughout the book the elusiveness and duplicity of language and provides continued illustrations of the modern grotesque. From the first sentence of the tale— "There is a story.—I cannot tell it.—I have no words"—Anderson firmly reestablishes the thematic terrain he mined in *Winesburg*.[4] With such tales as "I Want to Know Why," "The Egg," and "The Other Woman," he underscores the instability of telling an objective story by resorting to first-person narrators. In the first two tales he further obfuscates the possibility of conveying a truthful story through the use of retrospective narratives. These tales, as well as others such as "Unlighted Lamps," "The Door of the Trap," and "The New Englander," succeed in further developing Anderson's concerns for how individuals subject themselves to various forces in society, forces that range from the success myth, to marriage, family relations, and gender roles.

Lacking an introductory sketch, *Horses and Men* nevertheless follows a pattern, one of paired stories, with one set in the country and one in the city in each pairing. Whether framed in an urban or rural setting, though, each tale explores still other variations of the modern grotesque, with all of them involving the duplicity of language and the subjection of individuals to some facet of society. Continuing from "I Want to Know Why" in his earlier collection, Anderson completes his triad of first-person narrators in racetrack settings, narrators who yearn for understanding in "I'm a Fool" and "The Man

113

Who Became a Woman"; the latter is one of the most rewarding of Anderson's works that underscore instability of meaning—whether in the telling of a tale or in living in modern America. Also worthy of note are "Milk Bottles" and "The Sad Horn Blowers" for their depiction of characters who variously immerse themselves in delusions or resignedly accept feeling disconnected from modern life.

Ten years later, in his last collection of tales, *Death in the Woods and Other Stories,* Anderson further widened his canvas in depicting modern life in America. With the title story he reaches a culmination of sorts: fascinated with strong but defeated women since his first novel, he presents us with Ma Grimes. In addition, as in *Winesburg,* his first success in using purposely evasive narrators, he provides here another first-person narrator, who retrospectively tries to understand Ma Grimes's story in a self-conscious reconstruction of a past event. But other tales also warrant examination through a contemporary theoretical lens. In those like "The Return," "There She Is—She Is Taking Her Bath," and "In a Strange Town," Anderson presents us with updated portraits of the modern grotesque in three middle-aged men. With "A Meeting South," he provides an equivocal first-person narration of an illusory way of life in New Orleans that its inhabitants quite consciously prefer to any other alternatives. And in "Brother Death" he again reaches a culmination, as with George Willard and Helen White in *Winesburg*'s "Sophistication," where Ted and Mary Grey achieve an intuitive understanding. Many of Anderson's short stories after *Winesburg, Ohio* offer a veritable gold mine of fresh insights to anyone approaching them from the methodology employed in this book.

Finally, some of Anderson's long-neglected works—his quasi-journalistic accounts of industrialized America in the 1930s—deserve mention. In his travels throughout the South with Eleanor Copenhaver, Anderson was struck by what he saw as a dangerous alliance of the manipulation of the nation's success myth with an expanding modern technology. In works like *Perhaps Women* (1931), *Puzzled America* (1935), and the last work published during his lifetime, *Home Town* (1940), he attempts to address such issues head on without resorting to the artifice of fiction. These works function like complementary parts of a triptych; individually each may be flawed, but taken as a whole, they offer a provocative portrait of 1930s America.[5] Besides having obvious attractions for New Historicist and neo-Marxist critics, the three works would also be of interest to ideological and feminist critics. Ideological critics would find numerous instances in each work of Anderson's deconstructing the success myth and the very notion of "America"; feminists would find Anderson's solution to the emasculation of men in industrialized America—with the antidote of "perhaps women" (strong, independent women not distracted by society's prescribed roles for the sexes)—to be both compelling and vexing. But outside of glancing references in biographies, really very little has been done on these works.

This outline of further directions scholars may take with Anderson's works is intended to be thought-provoking rather than exhaustive. The author of the pamphlet in Melville's *Pierre* advises that the first of his 333 lectures is "not so much the Portal, as part of the temporary Scaffolding to the Portal of this new Philosophy";[6] so too should one regard these suggestions. The biographers' Sherwood Anderson, the New Critics' Anderson, the psychoanalytical critics' Anderson are all still alive and well and still provide valuable insights. This study has shown, however, that there are indeed many more Sherwood Andersons waiting to be discovered for readers of the new millennium. This book began with an epigraph taken from Anderson's *Memoirs:* "The time will come when . . . there will be a renaissance and then my own work and my own life will be appreciated."[7] Although both his work and his life have been appreciated, albeit with reservations, the time has now come for that renaissance in studying Sherwood Anderson's works.

115

NOTES

INTRODUCTION

1. Melville, letter to Nathaniel Hawthorne, June 1?, 1851, *Correspondence*, 193.
2. Lauter, "Melville Climbs the Canon," 1–24.
3. To illustrate, Sherwood Anderson is one of fewer than ten authors out of nearly four hundred to be given a major entry in the recent *Dictionary of Midwestern Literature*.
4. Shafer, ed., *American Literature*; Warfel, et al., eds., *The American Mind*; Bénet and Pearson, eds., *The Oxford Anthology of American Literature*, vol. 2; Simpson and Nevins, eds., *The American Reader*.
5. Davis, et al., eds., *American Literature*, vol. 2; Howard, et al., eds., *American Heritage*, vol. 2; Bradley, et al., eds., *The American Tradition in Literature*, shorter ed.
6. Perry Miller, ed., *Major Writers of America*, vol. 2.
7. Gottesman, et al., eds., *Norton Anthology of American Literature*, vol. 2; Baym, et al., eds., *The Norton Anthology of American Literature*, 5th ed., vol. 2; Poirier and Vance, eds., *American Literature*, vol. 2; McMichael, et al., eds., *Anthology of American Literature*, 7th ed., vol. 2; Lauter, ed., *The Heath Anthology of American Literature*, 4th ed., vol. 2; Baym, ed., *The Norton Anthology of American Literature*, 6th ed., vol. 2.
8. Blankenship, *American Literature as an Expression of the National Mind*, 665; Quinn, ed., *The Literature of the American People*, 872; Perry Miller, ed., *Major Writers of America*, 675.
9. Spiller, et al., eds., *Literary History of the United States*, 1233.
10. Sherwood Anderson, *Kit Brandon* (Arbor, 1985); *Poor White* (New Directions, 1993); *A Story Teller's Story* (Penguin, 1989); *The Triumph of the Egg* (Four Walls Eight Windows, 1988) and the same work but with altered title, *The Egg and Other Stories* (Dover, 2000); *Windy McPherson's Son* (Univ. of Illinois Press, 1993); *Winesburg, Ohio* (Bantam, 1995), (Barnes and Noble, 1995), (Dover, 1995), (Oxford Univ. Press, 1997), (Signet, 1993); *Winesburg, Ohio*, ed. Modlin and White (Norton, 1996); *Sherwood Anderson's* Winesburg, Ohio: *With Variant Readings and Annotations*, ed. White (Ohio Univ. Press, 1997).
11. Elliott, ed., *Columbia Literary History of the United States*. The recently released *Cambridge History of American Literature*'s volume on pre–World War II prose is a mixed

blessing for Sherwood Anderson. Edited by Sacvan Bercovitch, the volume is organized into three sections, a "cultural history of the modern American novel," the "story of the Harlem Renaissance," and "canonical texts and original immigrant writing." The section on the modern novel, written by David Minter, is further divided into twenty-seven subsections, with seven that single out individual authors (Henry Adams, Jack London, Ernest Hemingway, Henry Miller, Djuna Barnes, John Dos Passos, and William Faulkner). The work does not have a category into which Anderson is exclusively showcased. However, the references to Anderson's fiction and nonfiction that are scattered throughout this section, and especially a four-page treatment under the subsection, "The Perils of Plenty, or How the Twenties Acquired a Paranoid Tilt," which focuses on *Winesburg, Ohio,* provide a fresh overview of Anderson's work (130–33). Although Minter concludes that Anderson's status is that of a "flawed writer" (132), he does imply that Anderson was perhaps a budding deconstructionist, stating that *Winesburg* follows a "principle of fragmentation that pulls towards disintegration" (132).

12. Ennis, review of *A Reader's Guide to the Short Stories of Sherwood Anderson,* 12.
13. Lindsay, "'I Belong in Little Towns,'" 94.
14. Recent studies of the grotesque include Harpham, *On the Grotesque* (1982); McElroy, *Fiction of the Modern Grotesque* (1989); Russo, *The Female Grotesque* (1994); Meindl, *American Fiction and the Metaphysics of the Grotesque* (1996); and Cassuto, *The Inhuman Race* (1997). With the exception of Meindl, none of these critics even mentions Sherwood Anderson, and Meindl, whose coverage of American versions of the grotesque ranges from the mid–nineteenth century up to the present, gives him only cursory attention.
15. Anderson's reputation has benefited from a steady stream of criticism since his death, which was perhaps instigated by Lionel Trilling's rather dismissive 1942 essay on him published shortly after his death. See Trilling, "Sherwood Anderson."

1. ANDERSON'S GROTESQUES

1. For a historical and analytical assessment of the evolution of the grotesque, see Kayser, *The Grotesque in Art and Literature.* Meindl's *American Fiction and the Metaphysics of the Grotesque* also provides a concise overview of the grotesque, particularly 13–35.
2. Bakhtin's *Rabelais and His World,* for instance, concentrates primarily on the satirical and comedic qualities of the grotesque.
3. Harpham, *On the Grotesque,* 3.
4. Kayser, *The Grotesque in Art and Literature,* 124; McElroy, *Fiction of the Modern Grotesque,* 22.
5. Of course, even the belief that there was a preindustrial Golden Age for the individual in the United States is itself rather illusory. At the same time that writers like Emerson and Thoreau were championing self-reliance and nonconformity, for example, most Americans were preoccupied not with their inspiring prose but with self-help manuals and other works offering advice on how to acquire money and material possessions in

a competitive society. My point, though, is that by the end of the nineteenth century the belief in the autonomous individual had begun to wane in comparison to earlier decades.

6. McElroy, *Fiction of the Modern Grotesque,* 17.

7. Foucault, *Madness and Civilization,* 246.

8. Ibid., 249.

9. Ibid.

10. Ibid., 258, 267.

11. Foucault, *The History of Sexuality,* 53, 68.

12. Foucault, *Discipline and Punish,* 25–26.

13. Ibid., 202–3.

14. Ibid., 207.

15. Foucault, *History of Sexuality,* 92, 93.

16. Chase, *Sherwood Anderson,* 33.

17. Stouck, "Sherwood Anderson and the Postmodern Novel," 314.

18. Derrida, *Margins of Philosophy,* 9.

19. Ibid., 11, 13.

20. Ibid., 320.

21. Derrida would not subscribe, for instance, either to Gadamer's belief in a "true" (if perpetually evasive) interpretation of a text or to Gadamer's preference of verbal signs over written ones. Recognizing differences in their methodologies, David Couzens Hoy nevertheless finds common ground in both Gadamer and Derrida's belief in the "openness of language to new possibilities": "Both Derrida and Gadamer reject the possibility and utility of projecting a totalization of experience" (84). For a variety of critical interpretations of the "debates" between Gadamer and Derrida, see Michelfelder and Palmer, eds., *Dialogue and Deconstruction.*

22. Gadamer, *Truth and Method,* 306.

23. Ibid., 298.

24. Ibid., 388.

25. Ibid., 294, 340.

26. Ibid., 296, 395.

27. Melville, *Moby-Dick,* 434.

28. Some of the ideas in this section have evolved from my essay, "Beyond Grotesqueness in *Winesburg, Ohio.*"

29. Sherwood Anderson, *Winesburg, Ohio* (Oxford Univ. Press, 1997), 9. All references to *Winesburg, Ohio,* in this chapter will be to this edition, edited by Glen A. Love. In 1997 Ray Lewis White published what he called a definitive edition (*Sherwood Anderson's* Winesburg, Ohio), but it is actually plagued by numerous problems and is therefore unreliable. See my review and essay of White's edition, "The Book of the Grotesque: Textual Theory and the Editing of *Winesburg, Ohio.*"

30. Howe, for instance, faults "The Book of the Grotesque" for suggesting that "the grotesques are victims of their wilful fanaticism, while in the stories themselves grotesqueness is the result of an essentially valid resistance to forces external to its victims" (107).

Similarly, Ciancio faults the story because it "oversimplifies" the grotesques' dilemma: "It does not account for the external forces that contribute to [the] characters' grotesqueness or for the complications of their inward struggles" (994). Fussell simply dismisses altogether the importance of grotesqueness in the book, saying that "it is essential to . . . not allow ourselves to be tempted . . . to focus all our attention on the grotesques" (41).

31. Small, *A Reader's Guide to the Short Stories of Sherwood Anderson,* 25.

32. Among early commentators, Howe, for instance, argues that "the grotesques are distraught communicants in search of a ceremony, a social value, a manner of living, a lost ritual that may, by some means, re-establish a flow and exchange of emotion" (103). More vaguely, Cowley asserts that the grotesques' "lives have been distorted not . . . by their having seized upon a single truth, but rather by their inability to express themselves" (14). Rosenfeld puts it more bluntly, saying that the grotesques are "aged infants grown a little screw-loose with inarticulateness" (191).

33. Trilling perhaps unfairly reaches this conclusion about Anderson regarding his entire body of work (26).

2. THE EARLY NOVELS

1. Sherwood Anderson, *Sherwood Anderson's Notebook,* 196.

2. Harry Hansen, who knew Anderson during these Chicago years, recalls that Anderson brought four novels with him; of these the two that were never published were *Talbot Whittingham* and *Mary Cochran,* both of which are available in critical-edition dissertations by Gerald Nemanic and William Sanborn Pfeiffer, respectively (117).

3. Ibid., 122.

4. Sherwood Anderson, *Windy McPherson's Son,* 24. All references to *Windy McPherson's Son* in this chapter will be to this edition.

5. Scafidel, "Sexuality in *Windy McPherson's Son,*" 97.

6. Floyd Dell, who helped get the book published, recalls that Anderson originally had Sam acquire several more children en route to Sue but that he edited the conclusion (253). Anderson himself, not satisfied with the conclusion, later revised it for a 1922 edition of the book. See White, "The Revisions in *Windy McPherson's Son.*"

7. Sherwood Anderson, qtd. in White, introduction to *Windy McPherson's Son,* xxvii.

8. In one authorial aside, the narrator states:

> There is a widespread misunderstanding abroad regarding the motives of many of the American millionaires who sprang into prominence and affluence in the days of change . . . that followed the close of the Spanish War. They were, many of them . . . men who thought and acted quickly and with a daring and audacity impossible to the average mind. They wanted power and were, many of them, entirely unscrupulous, but for the most part they were men with a fire burning within them who became what they were because the world offered them no better outlet for their vast energies. (232–33)

9. Sherwood Anderson, *Marching Men*, 11. All references to *Marching Men* in this chapter will be to this edition.

10. Ditsky, "Sherwood Anderson's *Marching Men*," 111.

11. Lindsay, "The Unrealized City in Sherwood Anderson's *Windy McPherson's Son* and *Marching Men*," 21.

12. Rideout, "Talbot Whittingham and Anderson," 41.

13. As David D. Anderson has pointed out, Arthur Davison Ficke's collection of short poems, "Ten Grotesques," was published in the *Little Review* in March 1915, and Cloyd Head's experimental play, *Grotesques: A Decoration in Black and White*, was produced at the Chicago Little Theatre in November 1915. David D. Anderson, "*The Little Review* and Sherwood Anderson," 33. See also Townsend, *Sherwood Anderson*, 110.

14. Hansen, *Midwest Portraits*, 117.

15. Nemanic, "*Talbot Whittingham*," 15.

16. Without sufficiently explaining why, Rideout dates the novel's later composition to between spring 1914 and early summer 1915 ("Talbot Whittingham and Anderson" 42).

17. Reprinted in Sutton, ed., *Letters to Bab*, 584–88.

18. Ibid., 584.

19. Nemanic, "*Talbot Whittingham*," 272. All references to *Talbot Whittingham* in this chapter will be to this edition.

20. Rideout, "Talbot Whittingham and Anderson," 54.

21. Head, *Grotesques*, 31. All references to *Grotesques* in this chapter will be to this edition.

22. Atlas, "Experimentation in the Chicago Little Theatre," 12.

23. Ibid., 9.

24. Rideout, "Talbot Whittingham and Anderson," 57–58.

3. GETTING THE "THING NEEDED"

1. Eco, *Reflections on* The Name of the Rose, 66.

2. I am not arguing, though, that scholars have never addressed issues taken up here from a postmodernist perspective. In particular, several scholars have made insightful contributions to our understanding of how Anderson quite consciously draws our attention to both the indeterminacy of language and how language can be manipulated by those in positions of power to induce the submission of individuals. J. A. Ward argues, for instance, that as an advertising copy writer, "Anderson came to associate words themselves with lies; he used language for deceit and manipulation" (35–36). He continues: "The proper attitude towards words, as much as the book strongly indicates, is distrust. Words are indeed powerful even when meaningless, but they are also destructive" (44). In analyzing the failed attempts of the grotesques to communicate, Ward states, "Winesburg culture offers no acceptable mode of private communication. Dr. Reefy writes notes to himself, which he crumples in his pockets; other characters wave their arms, pace the streets, and get drunk—all improvised, inadequate substitutes for a speech that always fails them" (47). He correctly surmises that "inarticulation is the

121

only honest speech; silence must be the expression of truth, for the content of one's deepest desire is necessarily uncertain, unclear, and contradictory" (41).

Thomas Yingling has discussed the evacuation of meaning in language which writers like Anderson address: "Language itself is debased in the process of modernization. This debasement occurs not because words have changed but because their use is no longer what defines their value: As with all other commodities, it is only their circulation, their exchange, that 'counts'" (109).

Thomas Wetzel reminds us to take a cue from the evasive narration in determining the "truth" of the book: "This sense of the indefinite, the concealed truth, and the confused narrative pervades all of *Winesburg, Ohio,* calling the reader to read indirectly, away from the obvious and confused 'truth' of how the stories appear, and to look for different sorts of cues to find the essence of personal truth within Anderson's tales" (11).

Recalling Foucault's observations on normalized morality and the individual's subjection in society, David Mitchell points out how "the grotesque is constructed through a process of sublimation. To move from the nebulous world of possibility and multiplicity to the 'falsehood' of solidity entails a kind of moral error in Anderson's fictional world" (350).

Finally, Glen A. Love sheds new light on Anderson's "stylistic innovation" in the book, comparing it quite fairly to Hemingway's "iceberg theory": "Anderson . . . is deeply involved in techniques which leave the important things unsaid. Anderson's technique in this regard is to call attention, as narrator, to the inability of words to convey meaning satisfactorily" (xxii). And, in effect foreshadowing the arguments made in this study, Love contends that Anderson

> presents us, finally, with an important paradox, the artist who is, at bottom, sceptical of his medium: distrustful of words, he is nevertheless driven to their use, not only to record his scepticism, but also to attempt a communication which even at its best cannot approach the power of non-words, the more perfect communication which lies wrapped within purposeful silence. If this seems to suggest for the reader in a postmodern present something like a collapse of meaning and a retreat into interiority, then a further pondering of *Winesburg, Ohio* may be in order. (xxv)

Consider this study to be that "further pondering."

3. Fludernik, "'The Divine Accident of Life,'" 117; Rideout, "The Simplicity of *Winesburg, Ohio,*" 146.

4. Howe, *Sherwood Anderson,* 107.

5. Sherwood Anderson, *Winesburg, Ohio* (Oxford Univ. Press), 11. All references to *Winesburg, Ohio* in this chapter will be to this edition.

6. For years critics have debated whether Wing is a homosexual. First of all, if he did have sexual desires for his students he would be a pedophile and not necessarily a homosexual. But more to the point, it is not important to the story: the town, which

harbored suspicions about Adolph anyway, merely acts upon the "half-witted boy"'s words, which admittedly do not constitute a terribly reliable source. See Phillips about how Anderson purposely added phrasing to his descriptions of Wing in order to make his possible sexual disorder more suggestive than certain (31).

7. Arcana, "'Tandy,'" 67.

8. I also may be guilty of trying to "make sense" of a work that begs a coherent examination. One can plausibly argue, for instance, that the stranger's ideal conception of women is a resounding affirmation of Anderson's own ideal, as manifested in characters like Jane McPherson, Mary Underwood, and the unnamed prostitute in *Windy McPherson's Son;* Nance McGregor and Edith Carson in *Marching Men;* and perhaps, too, Elizabeth Willard in "Death." In this kind of reading, we would have to set the tale apart from all the rest because we would be accepting the facts and the telling of the tale at face value. But if we accept such a reading, we must return to the conclusion that "Tandy" is a weakly developed story, because Anderson so persistently causes us to question these two points throughout the book.

9. Ennis, "The Implied Community of *Winesburg, Ohio,*" 55.

10. O'Neill, "Anderson Writ Large," 67, 70.

11. Chase, *Sherwood Anderson,* 38.

12. Foucault, *The History of Sexuality,* 68, 83.

13. Rigsbee, "The Feminine in *Winesburg, Ohio,*" 235.

14. Rideout, "'The Tale of Perfect Balance,'" 243, 245.

15. Ciancio, "'The Sweetness of the Twisted Apples,'" 1005.

16. Fludernik, in "*Winesburg, Ohio,*" particularly 431–34, provides a fine, concise overview of the wide-ranging critical reception of George Willard's place in the book.

17. Jacobson, "*Winesburg, Ohio* and the Autobiographical Moment," 67.

18. David D. Anderson, "Sherwood Anderson's Moments of Insight," 158–59.

19. Fludernik, "*Winesburg, Ohio,*" 433. See also David D. Anderson, *Sherwood Anderson,* 49, and Fussell, "*Winesburg, Ohio,*" 45.

20. Phillips hypothesizes: "Whether a publisher suggested that the last stories ['Death,' 'Sophistication,' and 'Departure'] be written to round out the career of George Willard or whether Anderson felt that they were needed to make his 'Book of the Grotesque' [the original title of the book] something more than a mere collection of short stories cannot be determined" (37–38). Neither the precise date of composition nor Anderson's motivation behind writing "Departure" has been ascertained—although Small's conjecture that it was written "as late as 1918" (201) would suggest, if correct, why it may not be as fully developed a tale as the rest.

EPILOGUE

1. David D. Anderson, "The Structure of Sherwood Anderson's Short Story Collections," 91; Stouck, "Sherwood Anderson and the Postmodern Novel, 302–16; James Scott Miller, "Racial Limitations."

2. Townsend, *Sherwood Anderson,* 255–57.

3. Greasley, "Sherwood Anderson's Oral Tradition," 11; David D. Anderson, "Sherwood Anderson's Midwest and the Industrial South in *Beyond Desire*," 107, 108.

4. David D. Anderson, "The Structure of Sherwood Anderson's Short Story Collections," 92; Sherwood Anderson, *The Triumph of the Egg*, 1.

5. Robert Dunne, "Plainer Speaking," 94.

6. Melville, *Pierre*, 247.

7. Sherwood Anderson, *Memoirs*, 554.

BIBLIOGRAPHY

Anderson, David D. "*The Little Review* and Sherwood Anderson." *Midwestern Miscellany* 8 (1980): 28–38.

———. *Sherwood Anderson: An Introduction and Interpretation.* New York: Holt, 1967.

———. "Sherwood Anderson's Midwest and the Industrial South in *Beyond Desire.*" *MidAmerica* 26 (1999): 105–12.

———. "Sherwood Anderson's Moments of Insight." In *Critical Essays on Sherwood Anderson,* ed. David D. Anderson, 155–71. Boston: G. K. Hall, 1981.

———. "The Structure of Sherwood Anderson's Short Story Collections." *MidAmerica* 23 (1996): 90–98.

Anderson, Sherwood. *The Egg and Other Stories.* Ed. Charles E. Modlin. New York: Penguin, 1998.

———. *The Egg and Other Stories.* [*The Triumph of the Egg.*] Mineola, N.Y.: Dover, 2000.

———. *Kit Brandon.* 1936. New York: Arbor, 1985.

———. *Marching Men.* New York: John Lane, 1917.

———. *Poor White.* 1920. New York: New Directions, 1993.

———. *Sherwood Anderson's Memoirs.* Ed. Ray Lewis White. Chapel Hill: Univ. of North Carolina Press, 1969.

———. *Sherwood Anderson's Notebook.* 1926. Mamaroneck, N.Y.: Paul P. Appel, 1970.

———. *Sherwood Anderson's* Winesburg, Ohio: *With Variant Readings and Annotations.* Ed. Ray Lewis White. Athens: Ohio Univ. Press, 1997.

———. *A Story Teller's Story.* 1924. New York: Penguin, 1989.

———. *The Triumph of the Egg.* 1921. New York: Four Walls Eight Windows, 1988.

———. *Windy McPherson's Son.* 1916. Urbana: Univ. of Illinois Press, 1993.

———. *Winesburg, Ohio.* 1919. New York: Bantam, 1995.

———. *Winesburg, Ohio.* 1919. New York: Barnes and Noble, 1995.

———. *Winesburg, Ohio.* 1919. New York: Dover, 1995.

———. *Winesburg, Ohio.* 1919. New York: Oxford Univ. Press, 1997.

———. *Winesburg, Ohio.* 1919. New York: Signet, 1993.

———. *Winesburg, Ohio.* 1919. Ed. Charles E. Modlin and Ray Lewis White. New York: Norton, 1996.

Arcana, Judith. "'Tandy': At the Core of *Winesburg.*" *Studies in Short Fiction* 24 (1987): 66–70.

Atlas, Marilyn Judith. "Experimentation in the Chicago Little Theatre: Cloyd Head's *Grotesques.*" *Midwestern Miscellany* 8 (1980): 7–19.

Bakhtin, Mikhail. *Rabelais and His World.* Trans. Helene Iswolsky. Cambridge: Massachusetts Institute of Technology Press, 1968.

Baym, Nina, et al., eds. *The Norton Anthology of American Literature.* 5th ed. Vol. 2. New York: Norton, 1998.

———, gen. ed. *The Norton Anthology of American Literature.* 6th ed. Vol. 2. New York: Norton, 2002.

Benét, William Rose, and Norman Holmes Pearson, eds. *The Oxford Anthology of American Literature.* Vol. 2. New York: Oxford Univ. Press, 1947.

Bercovitch, Sacvan, ed. *Cambridge History of American Literature.* Vol. 6. Cambridge, U.K.: Cambridge Univ. Press, 2002.

Blankenship, Russell. *American Literature as an Expression of the National Mind.* 1931. Rev. ed. New York: Cooper Square, 1973.

Bradley, Sculley, et al., eds. *The American Tradition in Literature.* Shorter ed. New York: Norton, 1956.

Burbank, Rex. *Sherwood Anderson.* Boston: Twayne, 1964.

Campbell, Hilbert H., ed. *The Sherwood Anderson Diaries: 1936–1941.* Athens: Univ. of Georgia Press, 1987.

Cassuto, Leonard. *The Inhuman Race: The Racial Grotesque in American Literature and Culture.* New York: Columbia Univ. Press, 1997.

Chase, Cleveland B. *Sherwood Anderson.* New York: McBride, 1927.

Ciancio, Ralph. "'The Sweetness of the Twisted Apples': Unity of Vision in *Winesburg, Ohio.*" *PMLA* 87 (1972): 994–1006.

Cowley, Malcolm. Introduction to *Winesburg, Ohio,* by Sherwood Anderson. New York: Viking, 1960. 1–15.

Davis, Joe Lee, et al., eds. *American Literature: An Anthology and Critical Survey.* Vol. 2. New York: Scribner's, 1949.

Dell, Floyd. *Homecoming: An Autobiography.* 1933. Port Washington, N.Y.: Kennikat, 1969.

Derrida, Jacques. *Margins of Philosophy.* 1972. Trans. Alan Bass. Chicago: Univ. of Chicago Press, 1982.

Ditsky, John. "Sherwood Anderson's *Marching Men:* Unnatural Disorder and the Art of Force." *Twentieth Century Literature* 23 (1977): 102–14.

Dunne, Robert. "Beyond Grotesqueness in *Winesburg, Ohio.*" *Midwest Quarterly* 31 (1990): 180–91.

———. "The Book of the Grotesque: Textual Theory and the Editing of *Winesburg, Ohio.*" *Studies in Short Fiction* 35 (1998): 287–96.

———. "Plainer Speaking: Sherwood Anderson's Non-Fiction and the 'New Age.'" *MidAmerica* 19 (1992): 87–95.

Eco, Umberto. *Reflections on* The Name of the Rose. Trans. William Weaver. London: Secker and Warburg, 1985.

Elliott, Emory, ed. *Columbia Literary History of the United States.* New York: Columbia Univ. Press, 1988.

Ennis, Stephen. "The Implied Community of *Winesburg, Ohio.*" *The Old Northwest* 11 (1985): 51–60.

———. Review of *A Reader's Guide to the Short Stories of Sherwood Anderson,* by Judy Jo Small. *Winesburg Eagle* 20 (1995): 11–12.

Ficke, Arthur Davison. "Ten Grotesques." *Little Review* 2 (Mar. 1915): 31–35.

Fludernik, Monika. "'The Divine Accident of Life': Metaphoric Structure and Meaning in *Winesburg, Ohio.*" *Style* 22 (1988): 116–35.

———. "*Winesburg, Ohio:* The Apprenticeship of George Willard." *Amerikastudien* 32 (1987): 31–52.

Foucault, Michel. *Discipline and Punish: The Birth of the Prison.* 1975. Trans. Alan Sheridan. New York: Pantheon, 1977.

———. *The History of Sexuality.* Vol. 1. 1976. Trans. Robert Hurley. New York: Vintage, 1980.

———. *Madness and Civilization: A History of Insanity in the Age of Reason.* 1961. Trans. Richard Howard. New York: Random House, 1965.

Fussell, Edwin. "*Winesburg, Ohio:* Art and Isolation." In *Sherwood Anderson: A Collection of Critical Essays,* ed. Walter B. Rideout, 39–48. Englewood Cliffs, N.J.: Prentice-Hall, 1974. First published in *Modern Fiction Studies* 6, no. 2 (1960): 106–14.

Gadamer, Hans-Georg. *Truth and Method.* 2d rev. ed. Trans. Joel Weinsheimer and Donald G. Marshall. New York: Crossroad, 1989.

Gottesman, Ronald, et al., eds. *Norton Anthology of American Literature.* Vol. 2. New York: Norton, 1979.

Greasley, Philip A. "Sherwood Anderson's Oral Tradition." *Midwestern Miscellany* 23 (1995): 9–16.

———, ed. *Dictionary of Midwestern Literature.* Vol. 1. Bloomington: Indiana Univ. Press, 2001.

Hansen, Harry. *Midwest Portraits: A Book of Memories and Friendships.* New York: Harcourt, 1923.

Harpham, Geoffrey Galt. *On the Grotesque: Strategies of Contradiction in Art and Literature.* Princeton, N.J.: Princeton Univ. Press, 1982.

Head, Cloyd. *Grotesques: A Decoration in Black and White. Poetry* 9 (Oct. 1916): 1–32.

Howard, Leon, et al., eds. *American Heritage: An Anthology and Interpretive Survey of Our Literature.* Vol. 2. Boston: Heath, 1955.

Howe, Irving. *Sherwood Anderson.* Stanford, Calif.: Stanford Univ. Press, 1951.

Hoy, David Couzens. *The Critical Circle: Literature, History, and Philosophical Hermeneutics.* Berkeley: Univ. of California Press, 1982.

Jacobson, Marcia. "*Winesburg, Ohio* and the Autobiographical Moment." In *New Essays on Winesburg, Ohio,* ed. John W. Crowley, 53–72. New York: Cambridge Univ. Press, 1990.

Kayser, Wolfgang. *The Grotesque in Art and Literature.* 1957. Trans. Ulrich Weisstein. New York: McGraw-Hill, 1966.

Lauter, Paul. "Melville Climbs the Canon." *American Literature* 66 (1994): 1–24.

———, ed. *The Heath Anthology of American Literature.* 4th ed. Vol. 2. Boston: Houghton, 2002.

Lindsay, Clarence B. "'I Belong in Little Towns': Sherwood Anderson's Small Town Post-Modernism." *MidAmerica* 26 (1999): 77–104.

———. "The Unrealized City in Sherwood Anderson's *Windy McPherson's Son* and *Marching Men.*" *Midwestern Miscellany* 23 (1995): 17–27.

Love, Glen A. Introduction to *Winesburg, Ohio,* by Sherwood Anderson. New York: Oxford Univ. Press, 1997. vii–xxvi.

McElroy, Bernard. *Fiction of the Modern Grotesque.* London: Macmillan, 1989.

McMichael, George, et al., eds. *Anthology of American Literature.* 7th ed. Vol. 2. Englewood Cliffs, N.J.: Prentice Hall, 1999.

Meindl, Dieter. *American Fiction and the Metaphysics of the Grotesque.* Columbia: Univ. of Missouri Press, 1996.

Melville, Herman. Letter to Nathaniel Hawthorne June 1?, 1851. In *Correspondence,* ed. Lynn Horth, 190–94. Evanston, Ill.: Northwestern Univ. Press, 1993.

———. *Moby-Dick.* 1851. Ed. Hershel Parker, et al. Chicago: Northwestern Univ. Press, 1988.

———. *Pierre; or, The Ambiguities.* 1852. Ed. Harrison Hayford, et al. New York: Library of America, 1984.

Michelfelder, Diane P., and Richard E. Palmer, eds. *Dialogue and Deconstruction: The Gadamer-Derrida Encounter.* Albany: State Univ. of New York Press, 1989.

Miller, James Scott. "Racial Limitations: White Subjects, Black Others and the Legitimation of American Culture (1920–1950)." Ph.D. diss., Univ. of Wisconsin-Madison, 1998.

Miller, Perry, ed. *Major Writers of America.* Vol. 2. New York: Harcourt, 1962.

Mitchell, David. "Modernist Freaks and Postmodern Geeks." *The Disability Reader.* Ed. Lennard J. Davis. New York: Routledge, 1997. 348–65.

Modlin, Charles E., ed. *Certain Things Last: The Selected Short Stories of Sherwood Anderson.* New York: Four Walls Eight Windows, 1992.

———, ed. *Sherwood Anderson's Love Letters to Eleanor Copenhaver Anderson.* Athens: Univ. of Georgia Press, 1989.

Nemanic, Gerald. "*Talbot Whittingham:* An Annotated Edition of the Text Together with a Descriptive and Critical Essay." Ph.D. diss., University of Arizona, 1969.

O'Neill, John. "Anderson Writ Large: 'Godliness' in *Winesburg, Ohio.*" *Twentieth Century Literature* 23 (1977): 67–83.

Pfeiffer, William Sanborn. "An Edition of Sherwood Anderson's *Mary Cochran.*" Ph.D. diss., Kent State University, 1975.

Phillips, William L. "How Sherwood Anderson Wrote *Winesburg, Ohio.*" In *Sherwood Anderson: A Collection of Critical Essays,* ed. Walter B. Rideout, 18–38. Englewood Cliffs, N.J.: Prentice-Hall, 1974. First published in *American Literature* 23 (Mar. 1951): 7–30.

Poirier, Richard, and William L. Vance, eds. *American Literature.* Vol. 2. Boston: Little, Brown, 1970.

Quinn, Arthur Hobson, ed. *The Literature of the American People: An Historical and Critical Survey.* New York: Appleton-Century-Crofts, 1951.

Rideout, Walter B. "The Simplicity of *Winesburg, Ohio*." In *Critical Essays on Sherwood Anderson*, ed. David D. Anderson, 146–54. Boston: G. K. Hall, 1981.

———. "Talbot Whittingham and Anderson: A Passage to *Winesburg, Ohio*." In *Sherwood Anderson: Dimensions of His Literary Art*, ed. David D. Anderson, 41–60. N.p.: Michigan State Univ. Press, 1976.

———. "'The Tale of Perfect Balance': Sherwood Anderson's 'The Untold Lie.'" *Newberry Library Bulletin* 6 (1971): 243–50.

Rigsbee, Sally Adair. "The Feminine in *Winesburg, Ohio*." *Studies in American Fiction* 9 (1981): 233–44.

Rosenfeld, Paul. *Port of New York*. Urbana: Univ. of Illinois Press, 1961.

Russo, Mary. *The Female Grotesque: Risk, Excess and Modernity*. New York: Routledge, 1994.

Scafidel, J. R. "Sexuality in *Windy McPherson's Son*." *Twentieth Century Literature* 23 (1977): 94–101.

Shafer, Robert, ed. *American Literature*. New York: Doubleday, 1926.

Simpson, Claude M., and Allan Nevins, eds. *The American Reader*. Boston: Heath, 1941.

Small, Judy Jo. *A Reader's Guide to the Short Stories of Sherwood Anderson*. New York: G. K. Hall, 1994.

Spiller, Robert E., et al., eds. *Literary History of the United States*. 1948. 3d rev. ed., London: Macmillan, 1969.

Stouck, David. "Sherwood Anderson and the Postmodern Novel." *Contemporary Literature* 26 (1985): 302–16.

Sutton, William A., ed. *Letters to Bab: Sherwood Anderson to Marietta D. Finlay, 1916–33*. Urbana: Univ. of Illinois Press, 1985.

———. *The Road to Winesburg: A Mosaic of the Imaginative Life of Sherwood Anderson*. Metuchen, N.J.: Scarecrow, 1972.

Taylor, Welford Dunaway, and Charles E. Modlin, eds. *Southern Odyssey: Selected Writings by Sherwood Anderson*. Athens: Univ. of Georgia Press, 1997.

Townsend, Kim. *Sherwood Anderson*. Boston: Houghton, 1987.

Trilling, Lionel. "Sherwood Anderson." In *The Liberal Imagination*, 21–32. New York: Harcourt, 1950.

Ward, J. A. *American Silences: The Realism of James Agee, Walker Evans, and Edward Hopper*. Baton Rouge: Louisiana State Univ. Press, 1985.

Warfel, Harry R., et al., eds. *The American Mind: Selections from Literature of the United States*. New York: American Book, 1937.

Wetzel, Thomas. "'Beyond Human Understanding': Confusion and the Call in *Winesburg, Ohio*." *MidAmerica* 23 (1996): 11–27.

White, Ray Lewis. Introduction to *Windy McPherson's Son*, by Sherwood Anderson. Urbana: Univ. of Illinois Press, 1993. ix–xxxii.

———. "The Revisions in *Windy McPherson's Son*, Sherwood Anderson's First Novel." *Midwestern Miscellany* 12 (1984): 23–52.

———, ed. *Sherwood Anderson: Early Writings*. Kent, Ohio: Kent State Univ. Press, 1989.

———, ed. *Sherwood Anderson's Secret Love Letters: For Eleanor, A Letter a Day*. Baton Rouge: Louisiana State Univ. Press, 1991.

———, ed. *Sherwood Anderson's* Winesburg, Ohio*: With Variant Readings and Annotations.* Athens: Ohio Univ. Press, 1997.

Yingling, Thomas. "*Winesburg, Ohio* and the End of Collective Experience." In *New Essays on* Winesburg, Ohio, ed. John W. Crowley, 99–128. New York: Cambridge Univ. Press, 1990.

INDEX

131

134